HANDS-ON MATH

for Middle Grades

By Robert Smith

Illustrated by Jane Yamada

Edited by June Hetzel

Project Director: Sue Lewis

CTP ©1996, Creative Teaching Press, Inc., Cypress, CA 90630

Table of Contents

R=Reproducibles

Pages	Activity	Concepts

Reproducibles

Answer Key

Introduction

Each exciting activity in *Hands-On Middle Grade Math* includes two fun reproducible pages that tap into the students' mathematical curiosity and help them discover meaningful mathematical patterns and relationships. Journal Entries and Extensions assist students in extending and clarifying their learning. The activities are geared for grades 5–8. They are teacher- and student-friendly and have been successfully field-tested for years with middle grade students in Southern California.

Flexible, Hands-On Format

The hands-on format of the activities allow for a good deal of flexibility in teaching style. Some teachers prefer directed lessons and walking students through activities before allowing them to explore on their own. Other teachers briefly introduce concepts and then give students the duplicated pages, allowing them to explore the mathematical concepts independently. After independent exploration, the teacher reviews the concepts with the entire class to find out what discoveries the students have made in their independent exploration, encouraging students to clarify and refine their thinking and to think beyond their own solutions.

Grouping Techniques

Each activity lends itself to individual, partner, or cooperative group formats. Grouping techniques will vary from teacher to teacher depending on the type of class you have, the availability of materials, and your personal philosophy of teaching. Almost every activity can be done individually or in teams. Teams provide the opportunity for discussion and problem-solving with a partner. With more difficult or challenging material, pair a stronger math student with one who is either weaker in math or less able to read or follow written directions. Expect each student in a team to participate in each step of the activity. This serves to keep all students accountable and on task.

Manipulatives

Manipulatives are just as important in upper grades as in primary grades, but they are often harder to effectively adapt to middle grade concepts. The hands-on approach to math is crucial to internalizing the higher level concepts. This book provides clear, simple, and practical suggestions for effectively employing appropriate manipulatives at the grades 5–8 level.

Substitute where necessary for many of the manipulatives suggested in the activities. Corn kernels can be used for beans. Checkers or pennies can be used instead of plastic counters. It is important to provide variety because using different materials keeps students interested and involved.

Many math tools such as the compass, protractor, and calculator are integral parts of the activities. Provide ample time for students to become proficient using each mathematical tool. Skillful use of these tools will contribute to their success as mathematicians.

Open-Ended Processes and Solutions

Effective math teaching involves different approaches and different answers for some problems. The process is sometimes more important than the answer because the process involves the creative impetus of the child's mind. Encourage children to do all of the activities and to consider the open-ended extensions as the most important and most enjoyable of the activities. When specific and exact answers are called for, help students understand the importance of accuracy. The Answer Key at the end of the book is provided for your convenience.

Encourage your students to be creative in their approaches to the problems, to be less concerned with "Is this right?" and more concerned with seeking alternative, imaginative, or unusual approaches to solving the problems.

Tap Into Student Interest

To give students more open-ended discovery experiences, have them write their own problems for additional extension activities. This tends to engage the highest interest of the students because they take ownership of the problems, use their own names and ideas, and are involved in the solutions. It also tends to set the concepts firmly in place which is your basic goal.

Patterns . . . Patterns . . . Patterns

Your students will discover many patterns while participating in the activities in this book. Patterns are the language of math. Observation of patterns is one of the primary objectives in every math lesson. Good math students have been taught to look for patterns—what's alike, what's different, and what operation has been applied to one number to get another.

When mathematical talent and curiosity are nurtured, the routine processes and patterns of operations like multiplication and division become meaningful. Furthermore, using the operations in the context of real-life problems gives purpose to knowing when and how to apply these operations.

Across the Curriculum

The activities often integrate math with other disciplines, especially science and art, which serves to enrich both disciplines and to extend student understanding beyond the confines of one subject. Journal Entries allow students the opportunity to integrate their writing skills with mathematical concepts and to clarify their thinking.

We hope you will enjoy enriching your mathematics program through the use of *Hands-On Middle Grade Math*. This book will assist in stimulating the interest, enthusiasm, and growth of young mathematicians.

Marble Derby

Partner Activity

Concepts

Measurement, angles, use of protractor

Materials

Each pair of students needs:

- masking tape
- foam cup
- scissors
- marbles of various sizes
- protractor
- 3 rulers with grooves
- flexible clear plastic straws
- 2 small beads

Marble Derby

1. Tape two rulers together to form a hinge.

Journal Entry

What is the relationship between the angle of the ruler and the distance the cup moved? How does the angle of the ruler affect the speed of the marble?

---

2. Cut a foam cup in half and place it at the 6-inch mark of the right-hand ruler. The inside of the cup should face the inclined left ruler.

3. Hold the protractor perpendicular to the table. Lift the left ruler until it is at a 10° angle.

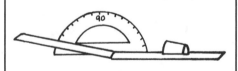

4. Place a marble in the groove at the top of the inclined ruler and release it.

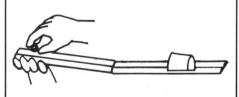

---

5. How many inches did the marble move the cup? Round to the nearest ¼-inch. Record the results on the chart below.

Angle	Inches Cup Moved
10°	_____
20°	_____
30°	_____
40°	_____
50°	_____
60°	_____
70°	_____
80°	_____
90°	_____

6. Move the ruler to a 20° angle, reset the cup at the 6-inch mark on the lower ruler, and release the marble as you did in step 4. Record your results. Continue this process, raising the ruler 10° each time. Stop when you get to 90°. What kinds of problems did you encounter (if any) between 60° and 90°? At which degree did the marble move the cup the farthest? Why did this happen?

Further Investigations

Marble Shooters

1. Tape three rulers together so that you have a 24-inch runway (two rulers) and one 12-inch ruler for inclination.

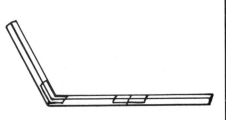

2. Place one marble (resting marble) at the 6-inch mark to allow 18 inches for the marble to travel.

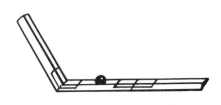

3. Lift the left ruler to a 10° angle.

Extension

Place three marbles at the 6-inch mark with the marbles touching each other. Release a marble from the top of the inclined ruler. Compare the movement of the three marbles with releases from various inclinations.

4. Place a second marble (moving marble) in the groove at the top of the inclined ruler and release it.

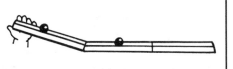

5. How many inches did the moving marble push the resting marble? Record your results on the chart.

Angle	Inches Marble Moved
10°	_____
20°	_____
30°	_____
40°	_____
50°	_____
60°	_____
70°	_____
80°	_____
90°	_____

6. Repeat steps 2 through 5 on page 6 using the angle settings in the chart. What is the relationship between the angle and the distance the resting marble moved?

Tubular Runways

1. Create your own tubular runways using straws taped to the rulers. Use beads instead of marbles and try various angles of inclination.

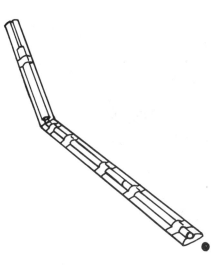

2. Tape the flexible straws together using angles of inclination to create the greatest momentum. Can you get a bead to go uphill?

Journal Entry

How does what you learned from Tubular Runways apply to roller coaster designs?

Footsies

Concept

Area

Materials

Each pair of students needs:
- 4–6 copies of reproducible graph paper, page 78
- pencil

Footsies

1. Take off one of your shoes. Place your stocking foot on a piece of graph paper with 1 cm squares. (You may need to tape two pieces of graph paper together.)

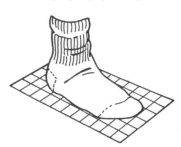

2. Have your partner outline your foot with a pencil.

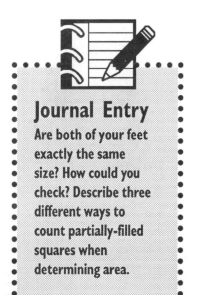

Journal Entry

Are both of your feet exactly the same size? How could you check? Describe three different ways to count partially-filled squares when determining area.

3. Count the number of square centimeters your foot covered.

4. Have your partner count the number of square centimeters your foot covered.

5. Compare your numbers. Do they agree? Why or why not?

6. Repeat steps 1–5 to determine the area in square centimeters of your partner's foot.

7. Share with other students your counting method and discuss which method(s) seem to be the most useful and accurate.

Counting Procedure

1. Try counting the square centimeter area of your foot using the following method (if it is one you and your classmates have not already discovered):

   a. Number in pencil every complete square on the graph paper that your foot covered.

   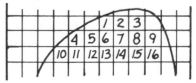

   b. Using pencil, number every partially-filled square and divide by 2.

   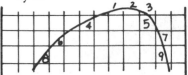

   c. Add the totals from a and b.

2. The final number is the area of your foot in square centimeters. How does this total compare with your Footsies' total?

3. What are the positive and negative aspects of this counting procedure?

Further Investigations

The Feet of Friends

1. Make a list of the foot areas of ten classmates. Use these measurements to make a bar graph like the one below:

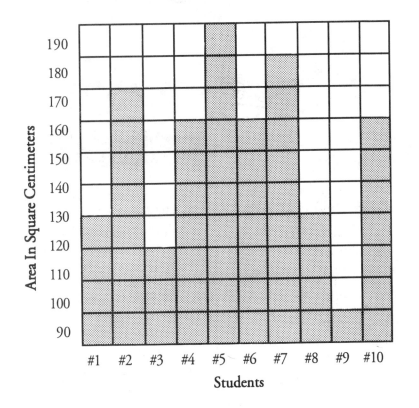

2. Is your foot larger or smaller than average for someone your age? Explain.

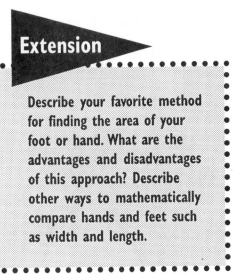
...And Handsies Too

1. Outline your left hand on the left side of a graph sheet. Keep your fingers together.

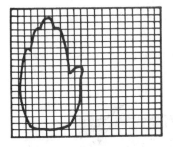

2. Count the area of your hand in square centimeters.

3. Make a list of the hand areas of eight other friends.

Tanya	120
Sally	131
Tom	129
Bill	138
Francesca	115
Sara	118
Amy	125
Jeremy	136

4. Create a bar graph to visually compare the hand sizes of you and your friends.

Journal Entry

Compare the area of your foot and your hand. How does this relationship (ratio) compare to those of your friends?

Straight Line Curves

Individual Activity

Concept

Geometry—properties of a line

Materials

Each student needs:

- ruler
- colored pencils or thin markers
- drawing paper
- compass

Straight Line Curves

1. Use your ruler to draw two straight lines 5 inches long in a V shape. The ends will not meet.

2. Mark dots ¼ inch apart along the length of both lines.

3. Number the dots 1 to 21 on the left line starting at the bottom.

4. Number the dots 1 to 21 on the right line starting at the top.

5. Use the ruler and colored pencils or thin line markers to connect like numbers on the left and right lines.

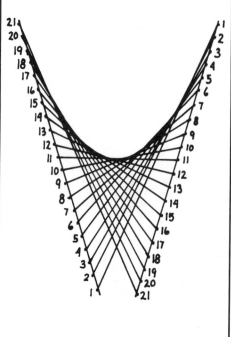

The Inverted "V"

1. Use your ruler to draw two lines in this 8-inch inverted "V" pattern. Do not let the ends meet.

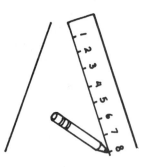

2. Mark dots ¼ inch apart along each line.

3. Number the left line 1 to 33 starting from the top and number the right line 1 to 33 starting from the bottom.

4. Use the ruler and colored pencils or thin line markers to connect like numbers on the left and right lines.

Journal Entry

After completing your line designs, describe the results. How could you extend this idea to create a complete straight line circle?

More Straight Line Designs

1. Use a compass to draw a circle with a 2-inch radius.

2. Mark dots ¼ inch apart all the way around the circle.

3. Number the dots on the circle. Put number 1 on one side of the circle and number 2 on the other side of the circle, but not directly across the center of the circle. Put number 3 above number 2. Put numbers 4 and 5 next to number 1 going below the circle.

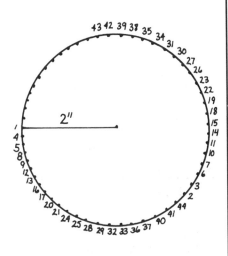

4. Follow the pattern shown on the illustration until you reach number 1 again. Leave the remaining dots unnumbered.

5. Use a ruler to connect the numbers sequentially—connect number 1 to number 2, number 3 to number 4, number 5 to number 6, and so on. Continue the pattern all the way around the circle including the unnumbered dots. Each dot should have two lines radiating from it.

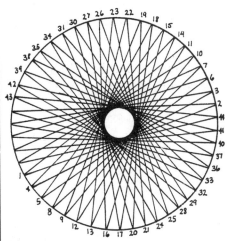

6. What pattern do you think you would get with the hexagonal figure? What would result if you tried an X-design? Give your reasons.

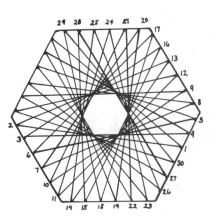

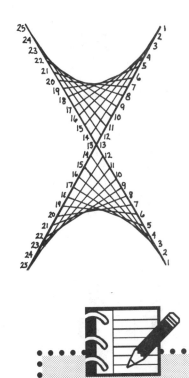

Extension

Create your own designs and numbering pattern with squares, pentagons, octagons, arcs, and other shapes.

Journal Entry

Why do you think the line designs create curved and circular patterns?

Rule of Six

Individual Activity

Concepts

Rule of Six, use of compass, use of protractor

Materials

Each student needs:

- ruler
- compass
- several pieces of plain drawing paper
- protractor
- pencil

Rule of Six

1. Practice drawing several circles with your compass. Become familiar with the feel and handling of this tool.

2. Set your compass setting at the 2-inch mark on the gauge or any other comfortable setting.

3. Draw another circle with the compass. Make sure the compass setting doesn't slip.

4. Put a dot anywhere on the circumference of the circle as shown below.

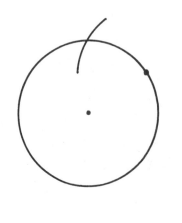

5. Put the sharp point of the compass on the dot you marked and draw an arc intersecting the circle.

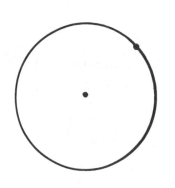

6. Place the point of the compass on the point you just made and draw another intersecting arc across the circumference of the circle.

7. Put another point at the new intersection and draw another arc.

8. Repeat this process until you have gone around the circle as shown.

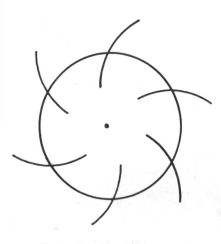

9. If you were exact and the compass setting did not change, the last arc should have gone directly through the first dot. This is the completed Rule of Six.

Journal Entry

Why would an artist or architect need to know the Rule of Six technique?

Further Investigations

Equilateral Triangles

1. The Rule of Six is used in many compass operations where geometric figures are inscribed within a figure.

2. Use a 2-inch compass setting or another comfortable setting and draw a circle.

3. Use the Rule of Six instructions on the previous page to divide the circle into six equal parts.

4. Letter the points of the circle A, B, C, D, E, and F.

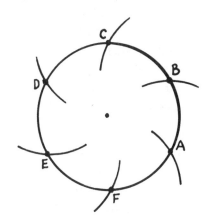

5. Use a ruler to draw line segments connecting points A and C, C and E, and E and A as shown. You have just drawn an equilateral triangle.

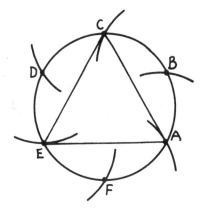

6. Equilateral triangles must have equal sides and equal angles. Measure your triangle to be sure it is drawn correctly.

More Rule of Six Fun

1. Use the Rule of Six to make a Star of David on a separate piece of paper.

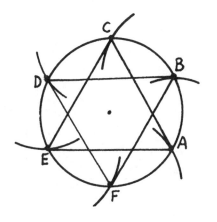

2. Use the Rule of Six to make a regular hexagon with six equal sides.

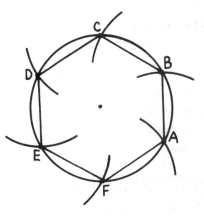

3. Use the Rule of Six to make a regular dodecagon with twelve equal sides.

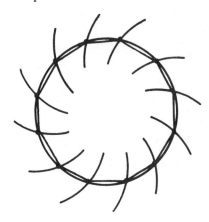

4. How many different angles can you find in the hexagon and dodecagon? Use your protractor to measure them.

Extension

How many equilateral triangles can you find in the Star of David? What other geometric figures can you make with your compass?

Journal Entry

What are some practical applications of the Rule of Six?

Flying Saucers

Individual Activity

Concepts

Concentric circles, radius, diameter, use of compass, Rule of Six, averaging

Materials

Each student needs:

- 3 file folders or 9" x 24" tagboard
- glue
- compass with pencil
- ruler
- 6 large paper clips
- scissors
- brad
- tape
- paper
- pencil
- measuring tape

Prerequisite Activity

Rule of Six, pages 12–13

Flying Saucers

1. Set your compass to a 4-inch radius.

2. The 4-inch setting allows you to draw a circle with an 8-inch diameter. 2r = d or "two times radius equals diameter."

Journal Entry

Describe places where you have seen concentric circles in nature.

3. Use the compass to draw a circle with an 8-inch diameter on a piece of posterboard, tagboard, or file folder. Cut out the circle.

4. Reduce the compass setting to a 3¹/₂-inch radius. Draw and cut out a circle that now has a 7-inch diameter.

5. Keep reducing the compass setting by ¹/₂-inch increments and drawing circles until you have eight circles.

6. Poke a hole through the exact center of each circle with the compass point.

7. Concentric circles share the same center point. Glue the circles together in a concentric pattern, smallest on top, largest on the bottom, keeping the center holes lined up.

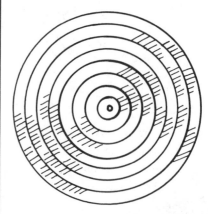

8. After gluing all eight pieces together, push a brad through the center hole and flatten the prongs on the back.

Further Investigations

Attach the Weights

1. Using the Rule of Six from page 12, mark the largest disk with six equally-spaced arcs.

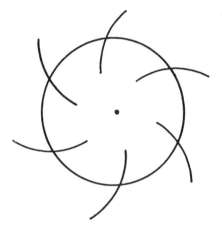

2. Place a large paper clip over each arc.

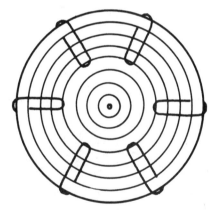

3. Tape the paper clips securely on the back of the largest disk. Tape the prongs of the brad also.

Fly the Saucer

1. Fly the saucer outside. Use a snap of the wrist to launch the saucer.

Caution:
Be safety conscious. Launch away from buildings and people.

2. Record and average six of your saucer's flight distances. How does your saucer's flight distance compare with a friend's?

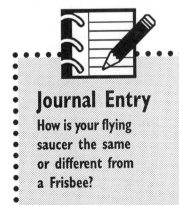

FlightVariables

1. Try flying the saucer with the wind, at an angle to the wind, and into the wind. How does wind affect the saucer's flight?

2. Try different throwing techniques. Which is most effective and why?

3. Try rearranging the weights. How does this affect the saucer's flight?

Extension

Brainstorm various ways to alter the design and create your own flying saucer.

Journal Entry

How is your flying saucer the same or different from a Frisbee?

Popcorn Pizzazz

Partner Activity

Concepts

Percentages, estimation

Materials

Each pair of students need:

- clear plastic cup ½ full of unpopped popcorn
- calculator
- clear plastic cup ⅓ full of water
- 1 teaspoon of baking soda on a paper towel
- clear plastic cup ⅓ full of vinegar
- stopwatch or clock with second hand
- paper
- pencil

Popcorn Pizzazz

1. Fill a plastic cup with ⅓ cup of water.

2. Add ⅓ cup of vinegar to the water.

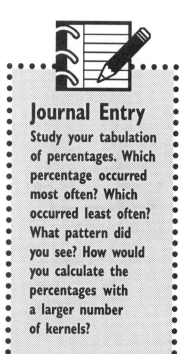

Journal Entry

Study your tabulation of percentages. Which percentage occurred most often? Which occurred least often? What pattern did you see? How would you calculate the percentages with a larger number of kernels?

3. Use your fingers to add three pinches of baking soda to the vinegar-water mixture.

4. Put two kernels of unpopped popcorn into the mixture. The kernels should start rising to the top and falling back down to the bottom of the cup. If they aren't rising, add another pinch or two of the baking soda. Do not add large amounts of baking soda.

5. Push the kernels down if they rise to the top and stay there. They should rise right back up.

6. Calculate the percentages of the kernels on the top like this:

   2 kernels on top - 100%

   1 kernel on top - 50%

   0 kernels on top - 0%

7. Keep a running tabulation recording the percentages of kernels on top at 5 second intervals. Record at least twenty percentages. Continue your chart on another paper.

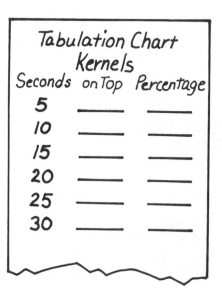

Tabulation Chart
Kernels

Seconds	on Top	Percentage
5	_____	_____
10	_____	_____
15	_____	_____
20	_____	_____
25	_____	_____
30	_____	_____

Further Investigations

Percentage Popcorn

1. Place 4 kernels in the cup of water/vinegar/baking soda solution.

2. Calculate the percentages this way:

   4 kernels on top - 100%

   3 kernels on top - 75%

   2 kernels on top - 50%

   1 kernel on top - 25%

   0 kernels on top - 0%

3. Make a tabulation chart like you did on the last page and record at least 20 percentages at 5 second intervals.

Extension

How would you calculate the percentages for larger numbers such as 15 or 20 kernels? What happens when you try to calculate numbers such as 7 or 13 kernels? Why would 100 total kernels be the easiest to compute?

Captain Kernel

1. Add 1 more kernel to the cup to make 5 kernels. Use the calculator to compute the percentages. Divide the number of kernels on top by the total number. (For example, 2 kernels on top divided by the 5 equals .4 or 40%.)

2. Tabulate 20 percentages with 5 kernels at 5 second intervals.

3. Add a couple more pinches of baking soda to pep up your mixture. Add 3 more kernels and use the calculator to compute percentages for 8 kernels. Keep a running tabulation as you did before.

4. Add 2 more kernels for a total of 10 kernels in the solution. Compute the percentages in your mind—1 kernel on top would be 10%, 2 on top would be 20%, 3 would be 30% and so forth.

5. Add kernels to the solution and use your calculator to compute the percentages for these totals: 12, 15, 20, and 25 kernels. Can you do some of these percentages just as fast without the calculator?

6. Describe the results of your tabulations. Did any percentages appear more often? Which percentages can you now calculate in your mind?

Journal Entry
List 10 ways to apply percentages to daily living.

Soapy Geometry

Partner/Individual Activity

Concept

Geometric shapes

Materials

Each team or student needs:

- straws
- thin insulated wire
- dish soap
- cooking oil
- water
- pail or tub (2½ gallon plus capacity)
- scissors
- measuring cup

Soapy Geometry

1. Thread thin insulated wire through straws to create these two-dimensional figures. Tightly twist the wire to stabilize each figure.

2. Stir 16 ounces of dish soap and 4 ounces of cooking oil into a bucket or tub with 2 gallons of water.

3. Dip your geometric figures into the soapy mixture and observe the bubbles created by the figures.

4. Experiment with the bubbles and film stretched across the faces of the figures (wave the figure through the air, touch the film with wet and dry hands, blow gently onto the surface of the film).

5. Try to make one shape inside another.

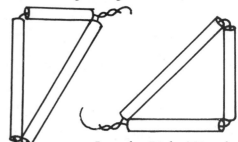

Right Triangle
(one 90 degree angle)

Isosceles Right Triangle
(90 degree angle and 2 equal sides)

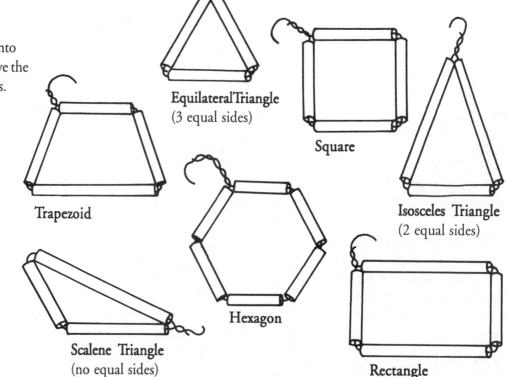

Equilateral Triangle
(3 equal sides)

Square

Trapezoid

Hexagon

Isosceles Triangle
(2 equal sides)

Scalene Triangle
(no equal sides)

Rectangle

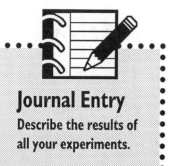

Journal Entry

Describe the results of all your experiments.

Further Investigations

Three-Dimensional Figures

1. Thread thin insulated wire through additional straws to create the illustrated three-dimensional figures. Twist the wire ends together to make each figure firm and tight. (Sometimes you will have to thread more than one wire through a straw to attach all of the straws.)

2. Dip the three-dimensional figures into the soapy mixture. Wave the three-dimensional figures through the air. Observe the soapy film and the bubbles created.

3. Touch the bubbles and film with wet and dry hands. Try to put your finger through the soapy film. What happens with each shape when you "blow" bubbles? Try to make one bubble inside another.

4. Count the *faces, edges,* and *vertices* (points) of each of these figures and record your information on the chart.

Figure	Faces	Edges	Vertices
Triangular Pyramid	_____	_____	_____
Square Pyramid	_____	_____	_____
Triangular Prism	_____	_____	_____
Rectangular Prism	_____	_____	_____
Cube (Hexahedron)	_____	_____	_____
Octahedron	_____	_____	_____

Triangular Pyramid

Square Pyramid

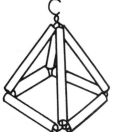

Triangular Prism

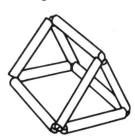

Rectangular Prism

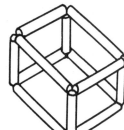

Cube (Hexahedron)

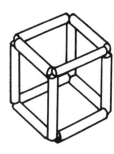

Octahedron

Extension

Use the wires and straws to create an isosceles right triangular prism and a scalene triangular prism. Experiment with these figures in the soap solution.

Journal Entry

Describe the bubbles created by each of the three-dimensional figures. What happened to the soapy film in these figures? What shapes were created inside these shapes? What kind of bubbles were made when you waved the soapy figure through the air? Were you able to put your fingers through the soapy windows without breaking the soap film? Could you blow bubbles through these figures?

Perimeter Pennies

Partner/Individual Activity

Concepts

Perimeter, area

Materials

Each student or pair needs:
- roll of pennies
- nickel, dime, quarter
- index card
- scrap paper/rectangular sizes
- reproducible, page 79

Penny Perimeters

1. Look at figures A and B on page 79. A perimeter is the measurement of the distance around the outside boundary of a figure. The formula for a rectangle is P = 2L + 2W or "perimeter equals two times length plus two times width."

2. To determine the exterior penny perimeter of figures A and B on page 79, count the pennies along the width and length, add them together, and multiply by 2. (Round to the nearest penny.)

Figure A
(4 + 5) x 2 = 18

Figure B
(4 + 3) x 2 = 14

3. Line pennies along the exterior sides of the width and length of an index card. Count the pennies on each side and add the numbers together.

4. Multiply by 2 to calculate the perimeter.

More Perimeters

1. Use pennies to calculate the perimeters of rectangular and irregular pieces of scrap paper. If the pennies don't exactly fit, round off each side to the nearest penny.

2. Record the perimeter in pennies for the following items:

Math book _____

Notebook _____

Magazine _____

Lunch box _____

Marker box _____

Your idea _____

Your idea _____

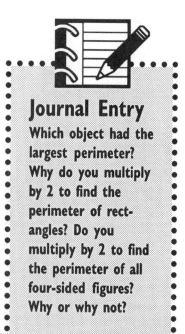

Journal Entry

Which object had the largest perimeter? Why do you multiply by 2 to find the perimeter of rect-angles? Do you multiply by 2 to find the perimeter of all four-sided figures? Why or why not?

Further Investigations

Making Cents of Area

1. Area refers to the number of square units inside a boundary. Cover Figure C on page 79 with equal rows of pennies. How many pennies does it take to cover the area of the figure?

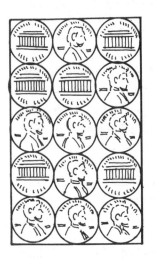

2. Count the number of pennies along the width and length of Figure C. Multiply length times width. Was the answer the same number as when you completely covered the figure with rows of pennies and counted them to obtain the area? A = l x w or "area equals length times width."

3. Cover Figure A and Figure B on page 79 with pennies. What is the area in pennies of Figure A? Figure B?

4. Cover an index card with pennies. What is the area in pennies?

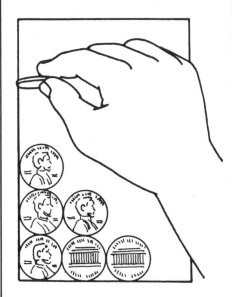

5. Using only one coin, compute the perimeter and area of each figure on page 79 in nickels, dimes, and quarters. Round to the nearest coin.

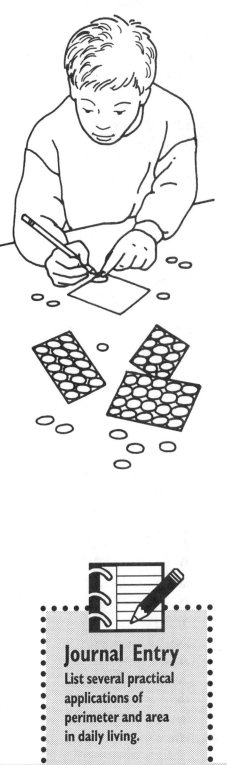

Cover Figure C on page 79

Extension

How could you determine the perimeter and area of your hand?

Journal Entry

List several practical applications of perimeter and area in daily living.

Square Coins

Partner Activity

Concept

Square roots, exponents, multiplication, division

Materials

Each pair of students needs:
- roll of pennies
- calculator

Square Coins

1. Make the smallest square you can with pennies. How many pennies did you use?

2. Make the next largest square you can with pennies. Be sure your square is filled in with pennies. How many pennies did you use?

3. Create a square figure with four pennies along one side of the square. How many pennies total? Be sure the square is completely filled with pennies.

4. Use a separate paper to draw pictures illustrating each of the squares created and to complete the chart below.

5. What is the largest square you could make with 3, 4, and 5 rolls of pennies (50 pennies per roll)?

6. Imagine that you had 1,000 pennies along one side. How many dollars worth of pennies would you need to complete the square?

Number of Pennies on One Side	Total Pennies in the Square
2 pennies	4 pennies
3 pennies	9 pennies
4 pennies	16 pennies
5 pennies	_____ pennies
6 pennies	_____ pennies
7 pennies	_____ pennies
8 pennies	_____ pennies
9 pennies	_____ pennies
10 pennies	_____ pennies

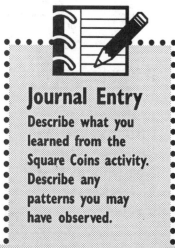

Journal Entry

Describe what you learned from the Square Coins activity. Describe any patterns you may have observed.

Further Investigations

Square Coins and Square Roots

1. There is a special way to write squared numbers. The small ^{2} next to the number being multiplied by itself is called an *exponent*. It is read as "2 squared or 2 to the second power, 3 squared or 3 to the second power, 4 squared or 4 to the second power, 5 squared or 5 to the second power," etc. 2^2 means 2 x 2; 3^2 means 3 x 3, etc. Look for the pattern below and complete the chart.

$2 \times 2 = 2^2 = 4$ $6 \times 6 = 6^2 = \underline{\hspace{1cm}}$

$3 \times 3 = 3^2 = 9$ $7 \times 7 = \underline{\hspace{1cm}} = \underline{\hspace{1cm}}$

$4 \times 4 = 4^2 = 16$ $8 \times 8 = \underline{\hspace{1cm}} = \underline{\hspace{1cm}}$

$5 \times 5 = 5^2 = 25$ $9 \times 9 = \underline{\hspace{1cm}} = \underline{\hspace{1cm}}$

2. Use your calculator to find the numerals these squared numbers represent.

$10^2 = 100$ $14^2 = \underline{\hspace{1cm}}$ $18^2 = \underline{\hspace{1cm}}$

$11^2 = 121$ $15^2 = \underline{\hspace{1cm}}$ $19^2 = \underline{\hspace{1cm}}$

$12^2 = \underline{\hspace{1cm}}$ $16^2 = \underline{\hspace{1cm}}$ $20^2 = \underline{\hspace{1cm}}$

$13^2 = \underline{\hspace{1cm}}$ $17^2 = \underline{\hspace{1cm}}$ $25^2 = \underline{\hspace{1cm}}$

Extension

Use your calculator to determine the square root of these numbers: 400, 900, 1600, 2500, 8100. Compute these square roots in your mind: 6,400; 4,900; 3,600; 14,400; 810,000; 25,000,000. What is the pattern? Describe how you calculated square roots in your mind. Compare it with your neighbors' approaches.

Square Roots

1. Use 9 pennies to make a square. One side should have 3 pennies. The square root of 9 is 3, or the number of pennies on each edge of the square.

2. Use 64 pennies to make a square. One side should have 8 pennies. What is the square root of 64?

3. Use pennies to make the squares shown on the chart below and determine the square root.

Number	Square Root
$\sqrt{25}$	_____
$\sqrt{81}$	_____
$\sqrt{100}$	_____
$\sqrt{121}$	_____
$\sqrt{144}$	_____
$\sqrt{169}$	_____

4. Use pennies to calculate the square root of 625. Check your answer with a calculator. You can do this by pressing 625 and then the radical sign ($\sqrt{}$).

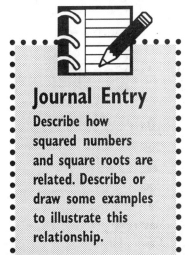

Journal Entry

Describe how squared numbers and square roots are related. Describe or draw some examples to illustrate this relationship.

Meniscus Mania

Partner Activity

Concepts

Measurement, liquid volume

Materials

Each pair of students need:

- 5 ml eye dropper
- water
- penny
- plastic cup
- nickel
- drinking glass
- dime
- coffee cup
- quarter
- saucer
- metric ruler

Meniscus Mania

1. Place a penny heads up on a flat surface. Use an eye dropper to put drops of water carefully on the surface of the penny.

2. Keep an accurate count of each drop you put on the penny. Measure and record the height of the "bubble" of water each time in millimeters. Continue adding drops until the water overflows.

Journal Entry

Which coins and sides held the most water and what techniques resulted in more water on the coins?

3. How many drops were you able to get on the penny? Record your results on the chart.

4. How high was the "bubble" that formed? The rounded surface is called a meniscus.

5. Repeat steps 1–4 using the coins listed. Record the number of drops you can fit on each coin and the height of the meniscus.

Meniscus Chart

	Number of Drops	Height (mm)
Penny/heads	_____	_____
Penny/tails	_____	_____
Nickel/heads	_____	_____
Nickel/tails	_____	_____
Dime/heads	_____	_____
Dime/tails	_____	_____
Quarter/heads	_____	_____
Quarter/tails	_____	_____

Further Investigations

Full and Overfull

1. Fill a clear plastic cup with water, level with the rim of the cup.

2. Put some water in another cup and fill your eye dropper with 5 milliliters of water.

3. Put the 5 milliliters of water in the full cup, one drop at a time.

4. See how many additional milliliters of water you can get into the cup before it overflows.

5. Perform three trials, record, and average your results:

   First Trial: _____ ml added to the full cup

   Second Trial: _____ ml added to the full cup

   Third Trial: _____ ml added to the full cup

   Average: _____

6. Were the results the same for each trial? How can we account for any differences? How did your results compare with your classmates' results?

Bubble Up

1. Make a meniscus with other containers. Fill each container to the brim with water and see how many additional drops you can add. Record your results below. Remember to multiply the number of droppers full of water by 5.

   Drinking glass: _____ ml

   Coffee cup: _____ ml

   Saucer: _____ ml

2. Describe the results of your investigations.

3. Water forms a meniscus because molecules of water have a tendency to stick to each other somewhat like magnets, especially on the surface of the water. How do you think this attraction makes it possible for insects to walk on water?

Extension

What happens to the meniscus if you put a few drops of dish soap or rubbing alcohol on it? What happens when you add other fluids? Try three or four additional fluids.

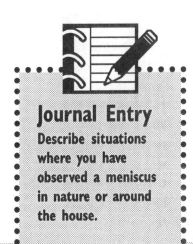

Journal Entry

Describe situations where you have observed a meniscus in nature or around the house.

Snail Sprints

Partner Activity

Concepts

Time, measurement

Materials

Each pair of students needs:

- 1 or 2 snails
- ruler
- plastic plates or bowls
- calculator
- newsprint paper
- water
- string
- watch
- pencil, paper
- tape measure

Snail Sprints

1. Obtain a snail from a moist area in your yard. Treat the snail gently.

2. Dip your snail in a shallow plate of water to get his "stomach-foot" wet or spray the snail with a fine-mist sprayer.

3. Choose a smooth, flat area for the race course such as a desk top or the floor. For best results, place a large piece of damp newsprint paper on the surface.

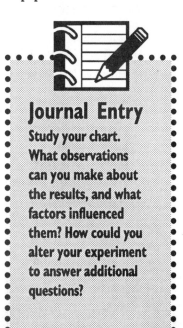

Journal Entry

Study your chart. What observations can you make about the results, and what factors influenced them? How could you alter your experiment to answer additional questions?

3. Mark a starting point. Place the snail(s) at that point. Use your watch or classroom clock to time your snail for one minute.

4. You can easily see the trail because the slime secreted by the moving snail is wet and dries glossy.

5. Place a piece of string along the winding trail following all of the turns made by the traveling snail.

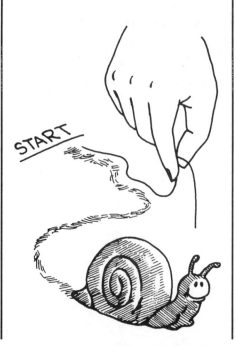

START

6. Measure the length of the string with a ruler to determine the distance traveled to the nearest inch.

7. Record the results on a chart. Measure and record at least 8 different one-minute trials. Try different surfaces (e.g., slanted surfaces) to see if results vary.

Trial Number	Distance Traveled
1	_____ inches
2	_____ inches
3	_____ inches
4	_____ inches
5	_____ inches
6	_____ inches
7	_____ inches
8	_____ inches

Creative Teaching Press/*Hands-On Math for Middle Grades*

Further Investigations

Snail Racers

1. Use a calculator to add the 8 distances traveled by your snail.

2. Divide the total inches traveled by 8 to calculate the average distance traveled by your snail in one minute.

3. Multiply this average number by 60 to approximate the number of inches the snail could travel in an hour. (For example, an average distance of 5 inches per minute would mean a speed of 300 inches per hour.)

4. Divide the number of inches traveled in 1 hour by 12 to convert the number of inches into feet. (For example, 300 inches divided by 12 would equal 25 feet.)

5. Calculate the speed of the snail in miles per hour by dividing the number of feet by 5,280 (the number of feet in 1 mile). (For example, 25 feet divided by 5,280 feet equals 0.0047348 or about .005 of a mile per hour.)

6. What was your snail's speed in miles per hour? About how many hours would it take to travel just 1 mile? (In the example above, it would take over 200 hours to travel 1 mile; 1 divided by .005 = 200.)

Extension

Do you think there are any animals slower than the snail? Did you notice any snails that traveled much faster than the others? Why do you think snails move the way they do? Compute the speed of another animal using the same method you used with the snail. Earthworms, ladybugs, slugs, pill bugs (roly-polys), ants, beetles, or caterpillars would be good choices for comparison and are fairly easy to find.

Walking Speed

1. Calculate your walking speed by following these steps.

   a. Mark a starting point.

   b. Walk for one minute at a comfortable pace.

   c. Measure the number of feet walked:

   _____

   d. Multiply by 60 to determine the number of feet you could walk in an hour:

   _____

   e. Divide by 5,280 to compute the miles you could walk per hour, assuming you walked at the same pace:

   _____

2. At the walking rate determined above, how long would it take you to walk across your state at its widest point?

   _____

3. At the same walking rate, how long would it take you to walk across the country at its widest point?

   _____

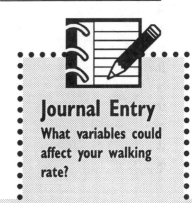

Journal Entry

What variables could affect your walking rate?

Your Weight on Mars

Individual Activity

Concept

Percentages

Materials

Each student needs:
- calculator
- paper
- pencil

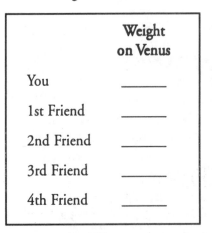

Your Weight on Mars

1. Surface gravity causes objects to feel heavy. Surface gravity is the force which pulls objects toward Earth. The surface gravity of every planet is different, depending on the mass of the planet and its distance from the object affected. Therefore, your weight would vary on each planet.

2. The surface gravity of Earth is the standard of comparison and is denoted as 1.00 or 100%. The surface gravity of other planets is then compared to Earth's by a decimal or percent. The surface gravity of Mars is only 0.38 or 38% that of Earth. If you weighed 100 pounds on Earth, you would weigh only 38 pounds on Mars (100 x .38 = 38).

3. Calculate your weight and the weights of four other friends if you were on Mars by multiplying each weight by 0.38. Record your results on the chart.

	Weight on Earth	Weight on Mars
You	___	___
1st Friend	___	___
2nd Friend	___	___
3rd Friend	___	___
4th Friend	___	___

Your Weight on Venus

1. The surface gravity of Venus is 0.90 or 90% of Earth's surface gravity.

2. Calculate your weight and the weights of four friends on Venus by multiplying each Earth weight by 0.90. Record each Venus weight on the chart below.

	Weight on Venus
You	___
1st Friend	___
2nd Friend	___
3rd Friend	___
4th Friend	___

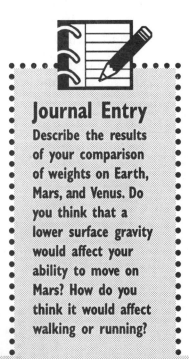

Journal Entry

Describe the results of your comparison of weights on Earth, Mars, and Venus. Do you think that a lower surface gravity would affect your ability to move on Mars? How do you think it would affect walking or running?

• Further Investigations

Our Solar System

Study this chart listing the surface gravity of all of the planets in our solar system:

Planet	Percent
Mercury	38% or 0.38
Venus	90% or 0.90
Earth	100% or 1.00
Mars	38% or 0.38
Jupiter	287% or 2.87
Saturn	132% or 1.32
Uranus	93% or 0.93
Neptune	123% or 1.23
Pluto	3% or 0.03

1. Calculate the weight of a 100 lb. person on each of the planets. Record your answers in the first column.

Planet	100 lb. Person	You	250 lb. Person
Mercury			
Venus			
Earth			
Mars			
Jupiter			
Saturn			
Uranus			
Neptune			
Pluto			

2. Calculate your weight on each of the planets and record the weights on the chart.

3. Calculate and record the weight of a 250 lb. person on each planet.

4. Describe your results and compare the weights of the three people on one of the planets.

Extension

Create your own solar system with nine planets. Name each planet and assign each one a different surface gravity. Calculate your weight on each imaginary planet.

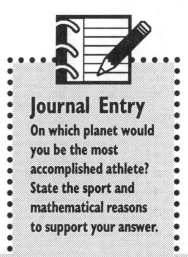

Journal Entry
On which planet would you be the most accomplished athlete? State the sport and mathematical reasons to support your answer.

Billionaire Blues

Partner Activity

Concepts

Time, large numbers, multiplication, calculator skills

Materials

Each pair of students will need:
- calculator
- pencil
- paper

Billionaire Blues

1. You have been given one billion dollar bills by an eccentric billionaire who made only two rules:

   - You may not spend any of the money until you have counted every single dollar.

   - You may only count for 8 hours a day. The rest of the time is spent eating, sleeping, and going to school as usual.

2. There are three facts you must know:

   - You can count 1 dollar every second.

   - There are 60 seconds in a minute.

   - There are 60 minutes in an hour.

3. Use your calculator to compute and record the number of dollars you can count in an 8 hour day.

Dollars Per Year

1. There are 365 days in one year.

2. Use your calculator to compute and record the number of dollars you can count in one year. (Remember, you can only count 8 hours per day.)

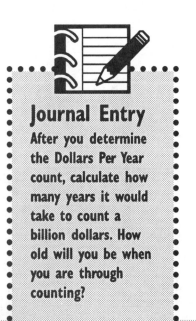

Journal Entry

After you determine the Dollars Per Year count, calculate how many years it would take to count a billion dollars. How old will you be when you are through counting?

• Further Investigations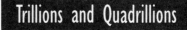

Billionaire Blues

1. Add a zero digit to the number of dollar bills you can count in a year to determine how many dollars you could count in 10 years. Record your number:

   _____

   You now have counted over 100 million dollars.

2. Record your estimate of the number you would use to multiply the above number by to get close to the billion dollar mark.
   Estimate: _____

3. Calculate the number of bills you could count in 50 years, 60 years, etc. Record the products for each calculation:

   50 years: _____

   60 years: _____

   70 years: _____

   80 years: _____

   90 years: _____

Calculator Hint:
Because a calculator only has room for 8 digits, drop the last 3 zero digits when you multiply, and reinsert the zeros after you finish your calculations.

Trillions and Quadrillions

1. A trillion dollars ($1,000,000,000,000) is one thousand times as much as a billion. How long would it take to count a trillion dollars?

2. A quadrillion dollars ($1,000,000,000,000,000) is one million times a billion. How long would it take to count this many bills?

Extension

Increase your counting speed to 5, 10, and 15 dollars per second. How would this affect the total counting time for a billion dollars?

946,080,000

Journal Entry
Plan a billion dollar budget.

Trophy Troubles

Partner/Individual Activity

Concept

Factorials

Materials

Each student or team needs:
- scissors
- calculator
- paper
- pencil
- reproducible, page 80

Trophy Troubles

1. Cut out the first two trophies, Most Considerate (MC) and Best Athlete (BA), from the reproducible on page 80.

2. How many different ways can you order the trophies? There are only 2 ways: either Most Considerate is first and Best Athlete is second or Best Athlete is first and Most Considerate is second.

3. Cut out the third trophy for Super Speller (SS).

4. Arrange the 3 trophies (first, second, and third) on your desk as many different ways as you can. Using abbreviations, create a chart to show the various arrangements.

MC	BA	SS
MC	SS	BA
BA	MC	SS
BA	—	—
SS	—	—
—	—	—

5. Cut out a fourth trophy (Best Coiffure or BC) and arrange all 4 trophies as many different ways as you can.

6. Record the different trophy arrangements on a chart. Here is the beginning of the chart:

MC	BA	SS	BC
MC	BA	BC	SS
MC	SS	BC	BA
MC	SS	BA	BC
MC	BC	SS	BA
MC	BC	BA	SS
BA	MC	SS	BC

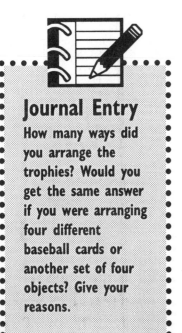

Journal Entry

How many ways did you arrange the trophies? Would you get the same answer if you were arranging four different baseball cards or another set of four objects? Give your reasons.

Further Investigations

More Trophies

1. Cut out the fifth trophy (Math Wizard or MW) and arrange all 5 trophies in as many different combinations as you can.

2. Carefully record each arrangement on a chart so that you don't repeat any. Use this model chart to get started.

MC	BA	SS	BC	MW
MC	BA	SS	MW	BC
MC	BA	BC	SS	MW
MC	BA	BC	MW	SS
MC	BA	MW	BC	SS
MC	BA	MW	SS	BC
MC	MW	BA	BC	SS
MC	MW	BA	SS	BC
MC	MW	BC	SS	BA
MC	MW	BC	BA	SS
MC	MW	SS	BC	BA
MC	MW	SS	BA	BC
MC	SS	—	—	—
MC	SS	—	—	—
—	—	—	—	—
—	—	—	—	—

3. Study the chart to find a pattern. Estimate the total number of permutations (arrangements) using a portion of the completed chart, and check the chart to see if it is reasonable. Give your reasons for choosing the estimate.

Working With Factorials

1. Examine the pattern:

   2 trophies 2 x 1 = 2 different arrangements

   3 trophies 3 x 2 x 1 = 6 different arrangements

   4 trophies 4 x 3 x 2 x 1 = 24 different arrangements

   5 trophies 5 x 4 x 3 x 2 x 1 = 120 different arrangements

   Problems like these are called factorials.

2. Cut out the last trophy (Student of the Year). Use the factorial pattern to calculate how many different ways 6 trophies could be arranged.

3. Use the factorial pattern to calculate how many different ways 7 trophies, 8 trophies, 9 trophies, and 10 trophies could be arranged. Does the factorial pattern always work?

Extension

You and your three siblings argue about who should sit where at the dinner table. Draw diagrams illustrating all the possible arrangements.

Journal Entry
List three practical ways to use factorials in everyday living.

Prime Picks

Individual/Partner Activity

Concept

Prime and composite numbers

Materials

Each student or team needs:

- marker
- 100 small cards or small paper squares
- calculator
- 2 index cards
- reproducible, page 81

Prime Picks

1. Number a deck of blank cards or small paper squares from 1 to 100 and arrange the cards in ten rows.

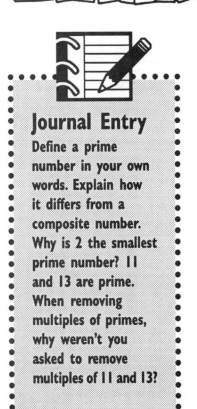

Journal Entry

Define a prime number in your own words. Explain how it differs from a composite number. Why is 2 the smallest prime number? 11 and 13 are prime. When removing multiples of primes, why weren't you asked to remove multiples of 11 and 13?

2. Make labels for two card piles by writing Composite Numbers and Prime Numbers on two index cards. You will be removing cards from the number arrangement and placing them in these two card piles. A prime number has only two factors: 1 and the number itself. A composite number has 3 or more factors.

3. Remove card 1 because that number is unique and does not belong in either pile.

4. Place number 2 on the prime pile. The only factors of 2 are 2 and 1.

5. Place every multiple of 2 (4, 6, 8, 10 . . . 100) in the composite pile since these numbers have at least 3 factors: 1, 2, and the number itself.

6. Place 3 on the prime pile since the only whole number factors of 3 are 3 and 1.

7. Place every remaining multiple of 3 (6, 9, 12 . . . 99) in the composite pile since these numbers have at least 3 factors: 1, 3, and the number itself.

8. Move 5 to the prime pile because its only factors are 1 and 5. Place every remaining multiple of 5 in the composite pile.

9. Move 7 to the prime pile because 7 and 1 are its only factors. Place every remaining multiple of 7 on the composite pile.

10. All remaining numbers belong in the prime pile. Count your prime numbers. You should have 25 prime numbers between 2 and 97. Your pile of composite numbers should have 74 numbers.

Further Investigations

Another Look

1. Number a deck of cards from 101 to 200 and arrange them as shown. Separate the numbers to prime and composite categories. Begin by removing the multiples of 2, 3, 5, and 7 as you did in the first activity. Then remove every remaining multiple of the prime numbers 11 and 13.

101	102	103	104	105	106	107	108	109	110
111	112	113	114	115	116	117	118	119	120
121	122	123	124	125	126	127	128	129	130
131	132	133	134	135	136	137	138	139	140
141	142	143	144	145	146	147	148	149	150
151	152	153	154	155	156	157	158	159	160
161	162	163	164	165	166	167	168	169	170
171	172	173	174	175	176	177	178	179	180
181	182	183	184	185	186	187	188	189	190
191	192	193	194	195	196	197	198	199	200

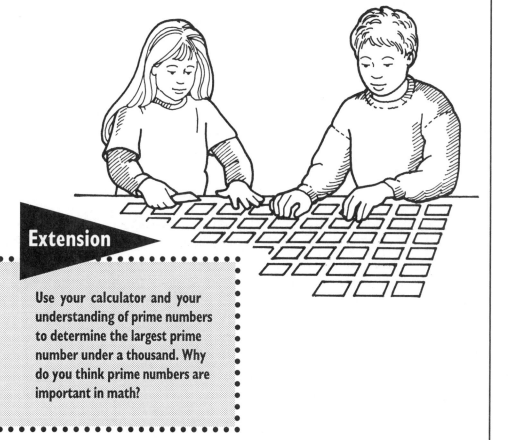

2. Be sure 143, 169, and 187 are on the composite pile. Count the primes between 101 and 200. How many prime numbers did you have?

3. Use the reproducible page on 81 to circle all of the prime numbers between 2 and 200.

4. Create a chart and use a calculator to determine the first multiple of 17 (over 200) you would have to remove using the method you learned in the first column on this page. (Remember all multiples of 2, 3, 5, 7, 11, and 13 would already be removed.)

Extension

Use your calculator and your understanding of prime numbers to determine the largest prime number under a thousand. Why do you think prime numbers are important in math?

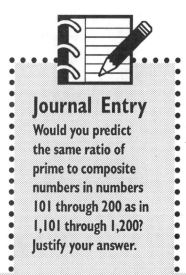

Journal Entry

Would you predict the same ratio of prime to composite numbers in numbers 101 through 200 as in 1,101 through 1,200? Justify your answer.

Toothpick Bases

Toothpick Bases

1. We use base ten in our everyday math. The base ten digits, going left from the decimal point, represent ones, groups of tens, groups of hundreds, groups of thousands, and so forth.

2. Other bases work similarly to base ten. Here is how base three digit values are determined:

   1s
   3s
   3 x 3 (or groups of 9)
   3 x 3 x 3 (or groups of 27)
   and so forth.

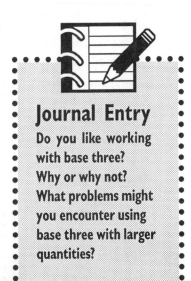

Journal Entry

Do you like working with base three? Why or why not? What problems might you encounter using base three with larger quantities?

Base Three

1. Let's practice with base three. Lay out 3 toothpicks. In base three, this would be written as 10 (base three). You read this as "one - zero, base three." It means that there is 1 group of three and 0 ones.

2. Lay out 5 toothpicks in the pattern shown here. In base three, this would be written as 12 (base three). You read this as "one - two, base three." It means that there is 1 group of three and 2 ones.

   /// //

3. Lay out 8 toothpicks in the pattern shown here. In base three, this would be written as 22 (base three). You read this as "two - two, base three." It means that there are 2 groups of three, and 2 ones left over.

   /// /// //

4. Try translating values from base ten to base three. Some of the problems are done for you. Illustrate each problem with toothpicks.

Base 10	Base 3
2	2
3	10
4	11
5	12
6	20
7	___
8	___
9	100
10	101
11	___
12	___
27	___
28	___
30	___
55	___

Notice that you can't write "3" in any given digit in base three just like you can't write "10" in any given digit in base ten ("1-0" fits in two digits).

27s	9s	3s	1s	
//		/	//	=

= 2012 (base three) or 59 (base ten)

Further Investigations

More Practice with Bases

1. Remember:
   - Base ten has 10 digits: 0, 1, 2, 3, 4, 5, 6, 7, 8, 9.
   - Base three has 3 digits: 0, 1, 2.
   - You cannot use the numeral 3 in writing base three numbers.

2. Arrange your toothpicks as shown here.

   /// /// ///

3. In base three, this is written as $100_{\text{(base three)}}$. You read it as "one - zero - zero, base three." It means that there is 1 group of nine and no ones.

4. Arrange your toothpicks as shown here.

   ///////// /// //

5. In base three, this is written as $112_{\text{(base three)}}$. You read it as "one - one - two, base three." It means that there is 1 nine, 1 three, and 2 ones.

6. Use your toothpicks to help you complete a chart like the one below.

Base Three Number	Toothpicks	Base Ten Number
$100_{\text{(base three)}}$	/////////	9
$101_{\text{(base three)}}$	///////// /	10
$121_{\text{(base three)}}$	_____	_____
$122_{\text{(base three)}}$	_____	_____
$222_{\text{(base three)}}$	_____	_____

7. Use your toothpicks to help write the following base ten values in base three: 29, 31, 36, 38, 44, 55, 64. How would your write a base three value for 1,000?

Extension

Complete the worksheet on page 82 for additional Toothpick Bases practice. How would you count in base two, four, or eight?

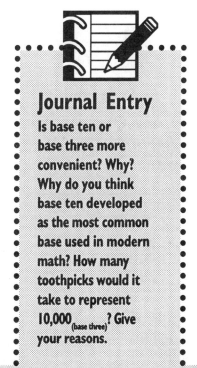

Journal Entry

Is base ten or base three more convenient? Why? Why do you think base ten developed as the most common base used in modern math? How many toothpicks would it take to represent $10,000_{\text{(base three)}}$? Give your reasons.

Corny Factors

Partner Activity

Concept

Factors

Materials

Each pair of students needs:

- clear plastic cup of uncooked popcorn
- calculator (optional)
- pencil

Corny Factors

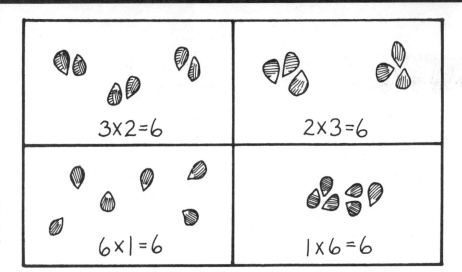

3 x 2 = 6   2 x 3 = 6

6 x 1 = 6   1 x 6 = 6

1. Count out 6 kernels of popcorn. Arrange them in 2 groups of 3 kernels. Arrange them in 3 groups of 2 kernels. You can also have 1 group of 6 kernels and 6 groups of 1 kernel each.

2. The factors of 6 are 1, 2, 3, and 6. The factorization of 6 can be written: 3 x 2, 2 x 3, 1 x 6, and 6 x 1.

3. Count out 12 kernels of corn. Arrange the kernels in the factor pairs show in the parentheses.

1 group of 12 kernels (1 x 12)

2 groups of 6 kernels (2 x 6)

3 groups of 4 kernels (3 x 4)

4 groups of 3 kernels (4 x 3)

6 groups of 2 kernels (6 x 2)

12 groups of 1 kernel (12 x 1)

4. Use the corn kernels to arrange as many factor pairs as you can for each of the numbers below. Make a chart and record the factor pairs below each number.

21	35	44	8	24	30
3 x 7					
7 x 3					
21 x 1					
1 x 21					

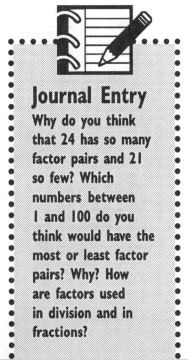

Journal Entry

Why do you think that 24 has so many factor pairs and 21 so few? Which numbers between 1 and 100 do you think would have the most or least factor pairs? Why? How are factors used in division and in fractions?

• Further Investigations

Corny Factors

1. Arrange 36 corn kernels in as many factor pairs as you can. List the pairs on a separate sheet of paper. Compare your pairs with your classmates' pairs. How many total factor pairs could you identify?

Extension

There are 360 degrees in a circle. This allows a circle to be broken into many different arrangements with equal parts. List all the factor pairs that you can find for 360. How many different ways can the circle be divided equally using whole numbers?

2. Find all the factor pairs for these larger numbers:

| 100 | 80 | 69 |

| 48 | 72 | 55 |

| 41 | 67 | 97 |

| 88 | 96 | 360 |

Compare your results with your classmates' results to be sure you have listed all the factor pairs possible for each number.

3. Describe any relationship(s) between the numbers 36, 72, and 360.

4. Arrange 19 kernels in as many factor pairs as you can. How many did you find? How many factor pairs can you discover in the following numbers?

| 23 | 11 | 31 |

| 41 | 67 | 97 |

| 5 | 17 | 29 |

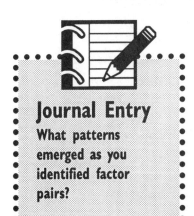

Journal Entry

What patterns emerged as you identified factor pairs?

Tetrahedral Pyramids

Individual Activity

Concept
Geometric solids

Materials
Each student needs:
- compass
- ruler
- protractor
- 9" x 12" drawing paper
- 9" x 12" tagboard
- scissors
- pencil

An Equilateral Triangle

1. Use your ruler to draw a 2-inch horizontal line segment on your drawing paper. Label the ends point A and point B.

2. Set your compass setting at exactly the length of line segment AB.

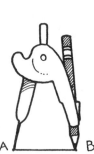

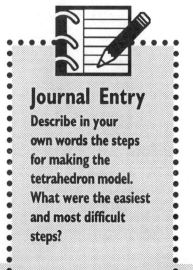
3. Place the point of the compass on point A and draw an arc above point A as shown.

A •————————• B

4. *Don't change the compass setting.* Place the point of the compass on point B and draw an arc above point B to intersect the first arc. Label the point where the two arcs intersect as C.

A •————————• B

5. Use your ruler to draw a line segment joining points A and C, and B and C. Measure each side of the triangle. They should be exactly the same length.

6. Use your protractor to measure each angle of the equilateral triangle. Each angle should measure exactly 60 degrees.

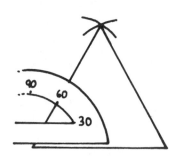

7. Practice making equilateral triangles of different sizes on your drawing paper. Try making some with sides as long as 5 inches and others as short as 1 inch. Check each one to see that the sides are equal and that the angles are exactly 60 degrees.

Further Investigations

Tetrahedral Pyramids

1. Use a ruler to draw a 2-inch line segment on the left side near the bottom of a piece of tagboard.

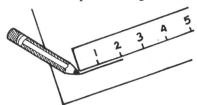

2. Create an equilateral triangle as you did on the first page of this activity.

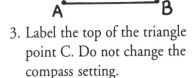

3. Label the top of the triangle point C. Do not change the compass setting.

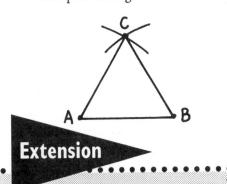

Extension

The ancient Greeks considered the equilateral triangle a symbol of perfection. What characteristics does the triangle have that might lead to such a belief? Where have you seen examples of equilateral triangles in buildings, art, advertisements, and other places?

4. Draw an arc from point C and draw an intersecting arc from point B as shown in the illustration. Label the point of intersection as point D.

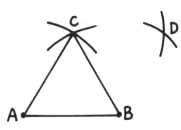

5. Use a ruler to draw straight lines connecting points C and D, and points B and D.

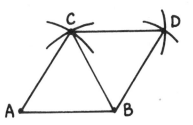

6. Without changing the compass setting, draw an arc from point B and an intersecting arc from point D. Label the point of intersection as point E.

7. Use a ruler to connect points B and E, and points D and E.

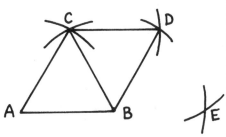

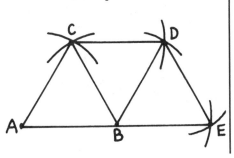

8. Without changing the compass setting, draw an arc from point C and an intersecting arc from point D. Label the intersection as point F.

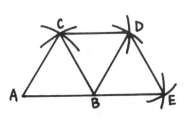

9. Use a ruler to connect points D and F, and points C and F.

10. Cut out along the outside edges. Fold along the lines (CD, BD, and CB) and tape the outer edges.

Journal Entry

How many equilateral triangles can you find in the tetrahedron model? What other geometric shapes can you find? How many faces, edges, and vertices does the three-dimensional figure have?

Flying Geometry

Individual Activity

Concept

Measurement, equilateral triangles

Materials

Each student needs:

- scissors
- ruler
- compass
- 9" x 12" tagboard or a file folder
- white glue or wood glue
- clear tape
- large paper clips
- reproducible, page 83
- pencil

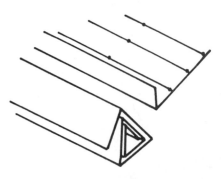

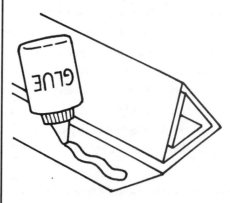

Flying Geometry

Note: The plane you will make has wings and rudder made entirely of equilateral triangles. The fuselage is made in the shape of a triangular prism. Use the pattern and reference drawings on page 83.

1. To make the fuselage or shaft of the plane, use a 5" x 12" piece of tagboard or a file folder.

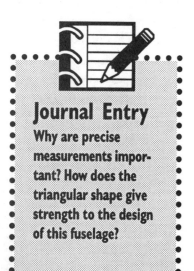

Journal Entry

Why are precise measurements important? How does the triangular shape give strength to the design of this fuselage?

2. With a ruler and pencil, use dots to carefully mark the following measurements in inches from one side of the tag: $\frac{1}{2}$, 1, $1\frac{1}{2}$, 2, $2\frac{3}{4}$, $3\frac{1}{2}$, $4\frac{1}{4}$, and 5.

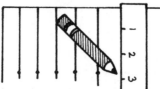

3. Move down a few inches on the tag and mark the measurements again. Use a ruler to draw straight lines through the corresponding dots. Make the lines the length of the tagboard.

4. Lay the ruler next to each line and trace the line with the point of your scissors. This will make the tagboard easier to fold.

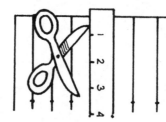

5. Fold the tagboard carefully along the lines along the $\frac{1}{2}$-inch marks, making a triangular prism and overlapping the rest of the layers. This will give the fuselage strength and an aerodynamic design.

6. Glue the last layer of the shaft to the one it overlaps and use clear tape to seal the shaft fold.

Further Investigations

Flying Geometry

1. Use your ruler to make a 6-inch line segment (AB) on the tagboard. This will be the base for an equilateral triangle.

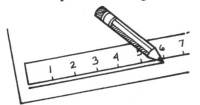

2. Set your compass the length of line segment AB. Place the point of the compass on point A and draw an arc above the line.

A _____ B

3. *Don't change the compass setting.* Place the point of the compass on point B and draw an intersecting arc above the line. Label the intersection point C.

A _____ B

Extension

Experiment with different shapes and sizes of shafts and wings to design the plane that flies the farthest. What did you learn? How does changing the angle of the rudder affect flight?

4. Use a ruler to draw a line from point A to C and from point B to C. Use a ruler to check that all three sides are equal. Cut out the triangle. This is the front wing.

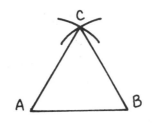

5. Use the same procedure to make a 3-inch equilateral triangle. This is the rear wing.

6. Use the same procedure to make a 2-inch equilateral triangle. This will be the rudder.

7. Make a mark at the 3-inch point on the base of the 6-inch triangle. Use the mark as a guide to glue the wing evenly onto the shaft. Be sure it is 2 inches from the tip of the shaft to the tip of the triangle.

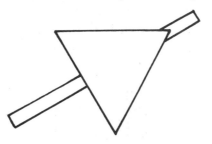

8. Glue the 3-inch triangular rear wing to the shaft even with the rear of the shaft.

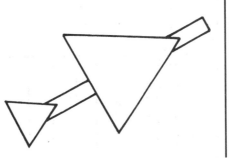

9. Fold the last 2-inch triangle ½ inch on one side. Attach it to the top of the rear wing as a rudder.

10. Tape all of the wings to make them secure. Let the glue dry. Place four or five large paper clips on the nose of the plane for weight.

11. Hold the plane behind the front wing or with a finger on the rear of the shaft and launch into the wind with a snap of the wrist. Experiment with your plane to see how to get it to fly the farthest.

12. Measure and record the distance of 6 to 8 flights. What is the average flight distance?

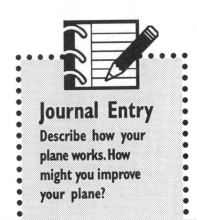

Journal Entry

Describe how your plane works. How might you improve your plane?

Oscillating Octahedrons

Individual Activity

Concepts

Octahedrons, use of compass

Materials

Each student needs:

- compass
- ruler
- drawing paper
- 8½" x 11" tagboard or manila folder
- markers or crayons
- clear tape
- fishing line or thin string
- coat hanger

Prerequisite Activity

Tetrahedral Pyramids, pages 40–41

Making an Octahedron

1. Use a ruler to draw a 2-inch horizontal line segment beginning at the far left side of a piece of tagboard or manila folder. The line segment should be halfway between the top and bottom of the 8½ by 11-inch paper.

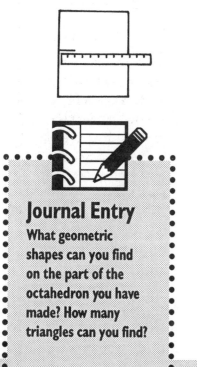

Journal Entry

What geometric shapes can you find on the part of the octahedron you have made? How many triangles can you find?

2. Follow the instructions on pages 40–41 for making a tetrahedron.

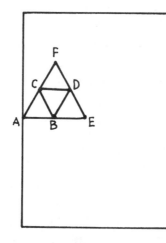

3. *Don't change the compass setting.* Draw an arc below point B as shown. Draw an intersecting arc below point E. Label the intersection point G.

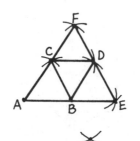

4. Use a ruler to connect point E to point G and to connect point B to point G.

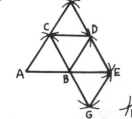

5. *Without changing the compass setting,* draw an arc from point E and an intersecting arc from point G. Label the intersection point H.

6. Use a ruler to connect point E to point H and point G to point H.

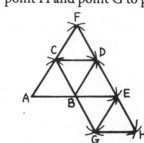

Further Investigations

Completing the Octahedron

1. *Without changing the compass setting,* draw an arc from point E and an intersecting arc from point H. Label the intersection point I.

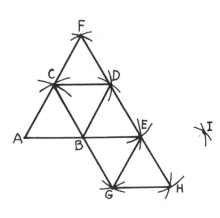

2. Use a ruler to connect point H to point I and point E to point I.

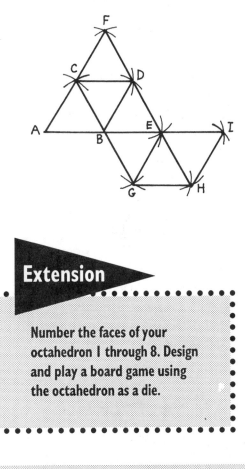

Extension

Number the faces of your octahedron 1 through 8. Design and play a board game using the octahedron as a die.

3. *Without changing the compass setting,* draw an arc from point G and an intersecting arc from point H. Label the intersection point J.

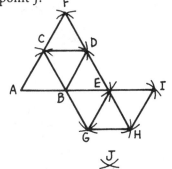

4. Use a ruler to connect point H to point J and point G to point J.

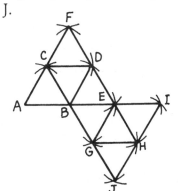

5. Use markers or crayons to give each of the eight triangles a different color.

6. Fold the octahedron carefully along the line segments. Use a ruler to get a sharper crease in your folds. Use clear tape to connect the edges of the figure.

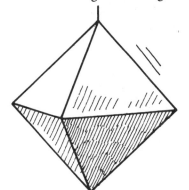

7. Examine your octahedron carefully. Why is it important to keep the compass setting the same for the entire figure? How many edges does this figure have? Are all of the edges exactly the same length? Are all of the faces the same size and shape?

8. Create another octahedron of a different size. Dangle the octahedrons from pieces of fishing line or thin string. Make additional geometric shapes and hang them from a coat hanger to create a mobile.

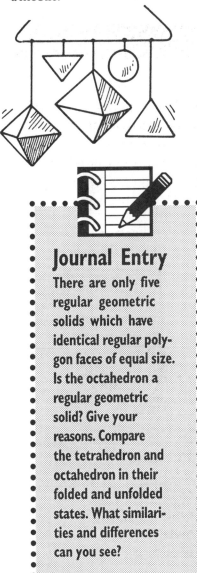

Journal Entry

There are only five regular geometric solids which have identical regular polygon faces of equal size. Is the octahedron a regular geometric solid? Give your reasons. Compare the tetrahedron and octahedron in their folded and unfolded states. What similarities and differences can you see?

Square Pyramids

Concept

Constructing perpendicular bisectors

Materials

Each student needs:

- ruler
- compass
- 8¹/₂" x 11" drawing paper
- scissors
- clear tape
- pencil

Constructing a Perpendicular Bisector

1. A perpendicular bisector cuts a line in half. The bisector is perpendicular to the line, creating four right angles.

2. Use your ruler to draw a horizontal line across a piece of drawing paper at about the middle of the paper.

Journal Entry

Write three rules for accurate use of the compass.

3. Use your ruler to mark a 2-inch line segment in the center of this line. Label the segment AB.

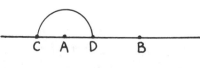

4. Set your compass at ³/₄ of an inch. Place the point of the compass on point A and draw a semi-circle above the line. Label the points on the line C and D as shown here.

5. Using the same ³/₄-inch compass setting, place the point of the compass on point B and draw a semi-circle. Label the points on the line E and F.

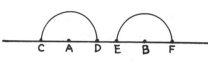

6. Make your compass setting 2 inches. Place the point of the compass on point C and draw an arc above and an arc below the line.

7. *Don't change the compass setting.* Place the point of the compass on point D and draw intersecting arcs above and below the line.

8. *Don't change the compass setting.* Place the point of the compass on point E and draw arcs above and below the line. Place the point of the compass on point F and draw intersecting arcs above and below the line.

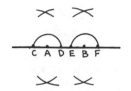

Further Investigations

Completing the Bisectors

1. Label the points of intersection W, X, Y, and Z.

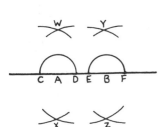

2. Use your ruler to draw a straight line through points W, A, and X. Draw another line through points Y, B, and Z. Both lines should extend more than 2 inches above line AB.

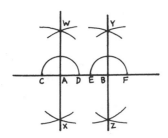

3. If your line doesn't go through each point, your compass slipped and you need to do the drawing over.

Extension

How could you make this figure using isosceles triangles?

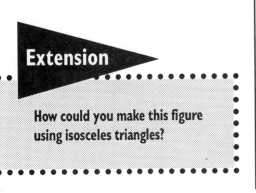

Completing the Square Base

1. Set the compass at 2 inches, the length of line segment AB. Set the point of the compass on point A and draw an arc above point A on line WX. Label the intersection point G.

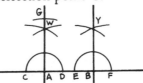

2. Do not change the compass setting. Put the point of the compass on point B and draw an arc above point B on line YZ. Label the intersection point H.

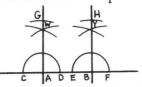

3. Connect point G to point H. Points A, B, G, and H form the base of the pyramid.

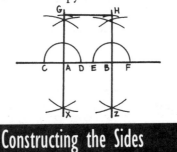

Constructing the Sides

1. Keep your compass setting at 2 inches. Set the point of the compass at point A and draw an arc to the left and up.

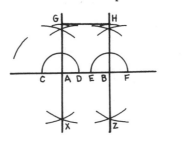

2. Set the point of the compass at point G and draw an arc to the left and down, intersecting the first arc. Label the intersection point I.

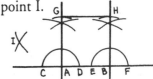

3. Use a ruler to connect point I to point A and to point G. This is the first triangular face of the pyramid.

4. Leave the compass setting at 2 inches and construct triangles the same way on the other three sides of the square base. Label points as shown.

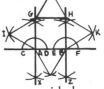

5. Cut out the pyramid along the triangular edges. Fold along the square edges and connect the edges with clear tape to form a pyramid.

Journal Entry

Why do architects and engineers have to know how to make perpendicular bisectors? How could you incorporate pyramids in building designs?

Cute Cubes

Individual Activity

Concept

Making hexahedrons

Materials

Each student needs:
- ruler
- compass
- 8½" x 11" (or larger) drawing paper
- tagboard or manila folder
- clear tape
- scissors

Prerequisite Activity

Square Pyramids, pages 46–47

Cute Cubes

Note: Make one or two practice figures on drawing paper before you do the cube on tagboard.

1. Use your ruler to draw a straight line across a piece of drawing paper about 3 inches from the top of the paper. Mark a 2-inch line segment in the center of this line. Label the segment AB.

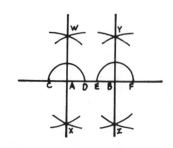

Journal Entry

What is the most difficult aspect of making accurate measurements and drawings?

2. Draw the perpendicular bisectors of line segment AB following the instructions for Square Pyramids on pages 46–47.

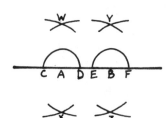

3. Use your ruler to draw a straight line through points W, A, and X. Draw a second line through points Y, B, and Z. The lines should extend more than 2 inches above and more than 6 inches below line AB.

4. If your lines don't go through each point, your compass slipped and you need to do the drawing over.

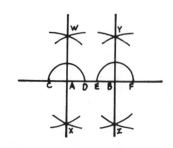

5. Set your compass setting at 2 inches, the length of line segment AB. Set the point of the compass on point A and draw an arc above point A on line WX. Label the intersection point G.

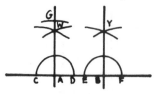

6. *Do not change the compass setting.* Put the point of the compass on point B and draw an arc above point B on line YZ. Label the intersection point H.

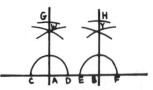

7. Use a ruler to connect point G to point H. This is the first face of the cube.

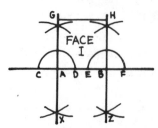

• Further Investigations

Completing the Cube

1. *Leave the compass setting at 2 inches for the rest of the construction.*

2. Place the point of the compass on point A and draw an arc below point A on line WX. Label the intersection point I.

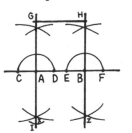

3. Place the point of the compass on point B and draw an intersecting arc below point B on line YZ. Label the intersection point J.

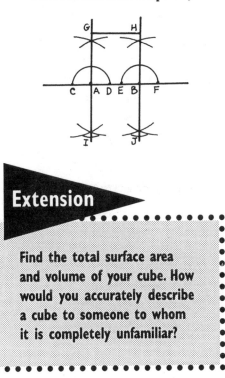

Extension

Find the total surface area and volume of your cube. How would you accurately describe a cube to someone to whom it is completely unfamiliar?

4. Use your ruler to draw a line through points I and J, extending 2 or more inches past each point. The second face of the cube is square ABJI.

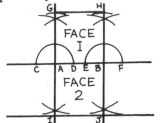

5. Draw an arc left from point A that intersects line AB. Name the intersection point K. Draw an arc left from point I that intersects line IJ. Name the intersection point L.

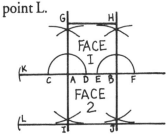

6. Use your ruler to connect points K and L. This creates the third face of the cube.

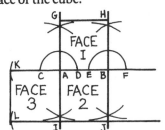

7. Use the compass to draw arcs to the right from points B and J. Use a ruler to connect intersecting points M and N to make the fourth face.

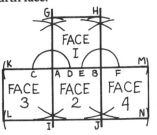

8. Place the compass point on point I and draw an intersecting arc below at point O. From point J draw an intersecting arc at point P. Connect points P and O to make the fifth face.

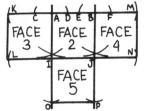

9. To make the last face, draw arcs below points O and P. Label the intersecting points Q and R. Connect points Q and R to make the sixth face.

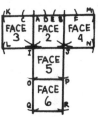

10. Use scissors to cut out the pattern. Fold carefully along the lines and connect the edges with clear tape.

11. How many edges, faces, and vertices does a cube have?

Journal Entry

Name as many objects as possible that use the shape of a cube in their design.

Dicey Dodecahedrons

Individual Activity

Concept

Geometric solids

Materials

Each student needs:

- ruler
- 9" x 12" tagboard
- reproducibles, pages 84–85
- clear tape
- crayons or markers
- scissors
- pencil

Dicey Dodecahedrons

1. A dodecahedron is a regular geometric solid with 12 pentagonal sides. The reproducibles on pages 84–85 have patterns of dodecahedrons which you can use when you make your own.

2. Find pentagon Y on the reproducible, page 84, Part I. Carefully cut out pentagon Y, place it on the edge of a piece of tagboard to avoid waste, and trace it exactly.

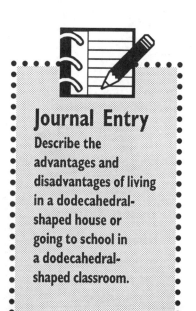

Journal Entry

Describe the advantages and disadvantages of living in a dodecahedral-shaped house or going to school in a dodecahedral-shaped classroom.

3. Cut out pentagon Y from the tagboard. Make sure that each side is exactly even and equal.

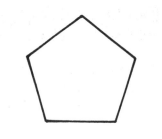

4. Study the pattern for the dodecahedron shown on page 85, Part II. Place the tagboard pentagon Y on a large piece of tag in the same location as pentagon A on the reproducible, page 85, Part II.

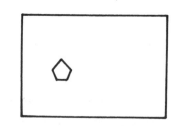

5. Carefully trace around the pentagon Y with your pencil. Relocate pentagon Y next to each side of pentagon A, tracing five additional pentagons. Label the six pentagons A through F as shown on page 85, part II.

6. Outline pentagon G next to pentagon F.

7. Outline pentagon H next to pentagon G. Pentagon H is the central pentagon of the second cluster of pentagons.

8. Outline and label the remaining pentagons I, J, K, and L.

Further Investigations

Dicey Dodecahedrons

1. Cut out the dodecahedron you have just traced from the tagboard.

2. Use crayons or markers to color each pentagon a different color.

3. Carefully fold and sharply crease every line between the pentagons.

4. Fold the edges up and tape the adjoining edges with clear tape. *Do not overlap any edges.*

5. Examine your dodecahedron. Count the number of faces. Count the edges. Count the vertices (points).

6. If you have completed pages 40–41 and 44–51, you have made four of the five regular geometric solids. Examine your models of each one and complete a chart like the one shown here.

	Tetrahedron	Octahedron	Cube	Dodecahedron
Faces	_____	_____	_____	_____
Edges	_____	_____	_____	_____
Vertices	_____	_____	_____	_____

Dodecahedral Die

1. Use the smallest pentagon model on page 84, Part I, to make a dodecahedron to use as a die. Be extremely careful in measuring and cutting.

2. Number each of the sides 1 through 12 before taping the dodecahedron's edges.

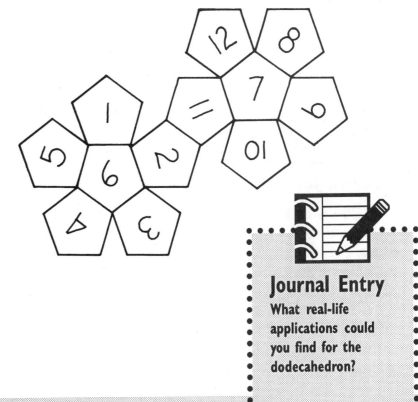

Extension

Roll the dodecahedral die 60 times and record the number that comes up each time. Before making the rolls, predict the results. Do you think the numbers will come up about equal in frequency or will some numbers be rolled more often? How did your results compare with your predictions? Save the die to use in other activities.

Journal Entry

What real-life applications could you find for the dodecahedron?

Heads Up

Concepts

Probability, graphing

Materials

Each student needs:

- a penny
- a pair of dice
- reproducibles, pages 86–87
- pencil

Heads Up

1. Predict the number of times you think heads will land up if you were to flip a penny 48 times. Record your prediction.

2. Flip a penny 48 times. Each time you flip the penny, record "H" for heads or "T" for tails in column one on page 86.

3. Count and record the total number of times it landed heads and the total number of times it landed tails. How did the results compare with your prediction?

4. Collect the results of nine of your friends and make a line graph like the one below. Use the grid on page 87 to show the number of times heads landed up.

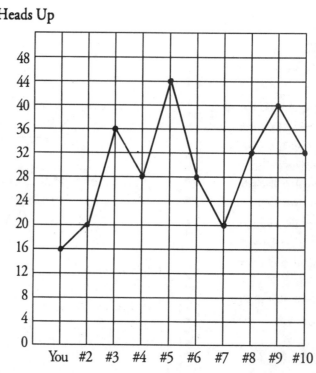

Journal Entry

What were the odds or probability of flipping heads? How close did you come? What happens when you combine your results with a group of friends?

• Further Investigations

Bar Graph

1. Roll one die 48 times and record in column two of the reproducible which number came up each time.

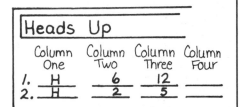

Heads Up			
Column One	Column Two	Column Three	Column Four
1. H	6	12	
2. H	2	5	

2. Tabulate the results and record on the back of your paper which number was rolled the most and least often.

1 – 10   4 – 9
2 – 5   5 – 6
3 – 12   6 – 6

3. Create a bar graph to illustrate your results. Give your graph a title and accurately label each axis.

DICE TOTALS

Extension

Roll three dice 48 times and record totals in column four of page 86. Make a graph using a copy of page 87 to illustrate the results of your investigations. Describe the results of your graph and explain why it might have turned out this way. What relationships do you see between the four columns on the reproducible?

Heads Up

1. Roll two dice 48 times and record the total for each roll in column three of the reproducible sheet.

Heads Up			
Column One	Column Two	Column Three	Column Four
1. H	6	12	13
2. H	2	5	7

2. Make a bar graph to illustrate the results of your investigation.

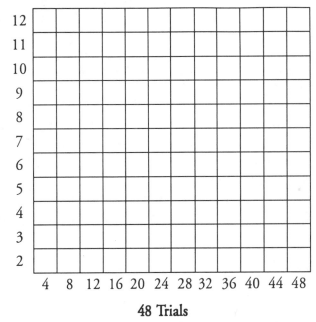

Sum of 2 Dice Rolled

48 Trials

3. Draw a freehand curving line across the top of your scores on the graph. Look for a pattern. Describe the pattern to a friend.

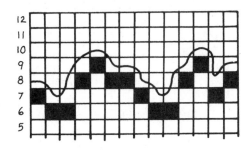

4. Compare your graph with those of your friends. Are there any similarities in the curves? Make a list of the numbers which were rolled most often by you and your friends.

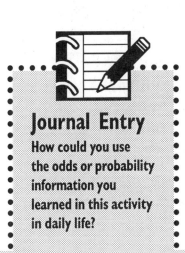

Journal Entry

How could you use the odds or probability information you learned in this activity in daily life?

Buggy Math

Concepts

Measurement, percentages

Materials

Each team or student needs:

- cricket (or a similar insect)
- metric ruler
- ladybug or other insect (optional)
- calculator
- reproducible, page 88
- pencil
- clear plastic cups (optional)

Buggy Math

Note to teacher: Crickets can be purchased inexpensively from pet stores and ladybugs are sold in garden stores. Review with students the importance of showing respect towards all living things before beginning this activity.

1. Carefully examine your cricket. You can do this by keeping it in an inverted clear plastic cup or *carefully* holding the insect with your thumb and forefinger.

Journal Entry

Compare notes with another student and describe any mathematical relationships that you noticed about the cricket's measurements.

2. Examine the sketch of the cricket on page 88 to locate and name the various parts of the body.

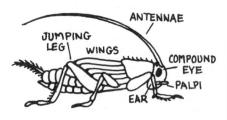

3. Use a metric ruler to measure in millimeters each of the body parts listed. Record your measurements on page 88. Because the insect can be active, you may have to estimate some measurements.

```
CRICKET BODY PARTS

JUMPING LEGS — 2 cm
ANTENNAE — 5 cm
BODY — 4 cm
FRONT LEGS —
WINGS ——
```

4. Discuss the results of your measurements with a partner.

- Did your cricket's left and right antennae vary in length?

- Could you tell if your cricket favored one antenna more than the other?

- Which pair of legs were the longest and which were the shortest?

- Which was the longest body section: head, thorax, or abdomen?

- What was the diameter (distance across) of the compound eye?

- Study the legs. How far do you think your cricket could jump?

Further Investigations

Buggy Math

1. The average length of a cricket's body is about 20 millimeters. The average length of its cercus is about 10 millimeters. As a fraction, the cercus is $^{10}/_{20}$ or $^1/_2$ of the body length. It is 50% of the length.

2. Examine your chart from page 88. Compute the fractional relationship of each body part to the cricket's length and record the fraction in column three of the reproducible. Use the measurement of the body part as the numerator and the total length of the cricket as the denominator.

3. Use a calculator to compute the percentage of each part of the cricket compared to its length. The percentage is calculated by dividing the numerator (top number) of the fraction by the denominator (bottom number). This is the same as dividing each body part by the length (e.g., 10 divided by 20 is .50 or 50%). Record the results in the last column of the chart on the reproducible.

Bug Number Contemplation

1. Were any parts of the cricket actually longer than the body?

2. Did you have fractions with larger numerators than denominators which could be reduced to mixed numbers and produce percentages over 100%?

3. Combine the length of the head and thorax. How does this total compare to the length of the body? Use a fraction and a percent to express the comparison (ratio).

4. Did the hind wings of your cricket extend beyond the rear of the body?

5. The average cricket can jump about 30 times its own length. About how far can your cricket jump? How does the distance your cricket jumps compare to its total body length?

Extension

Use another insect such as a ladybug, a silkworm moth, a grasshopper, or a baby cricket and make a chart like the one on page 88. Record the length of all of the insect's features. Compare the features of this insect to its total length in fractions and percentages. What are your observations?

Journal Entry

Which percentage did you find most surprising? Give your reasons.

Tangram Teasers

Individual/Partner Activity

Concepts

Tangrams, geometric relationships

Materials

Each student or team needs:

- posterboard
- ruler
- protractor
- reproducible, page 89
- drawing paper
- scissors
- tape

Tangram Teasers

1. Carefully cut out the seven tangram shapes illustrated on page 89 and tape these shapes onto a piece of stiff cardboard or posterboard.

2. Carefully cut out the shapes from the heavy board.

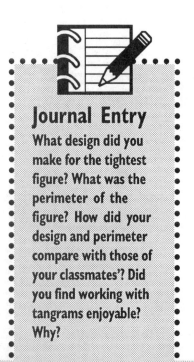

Journal Entry

What design did you make for the tightest figure? What was the perimeter of the figure? How did your design and perimeter compare with those of your classmates? Did you find working with tangrams enjoyable? Why?

3. An isosceles right triangle has a right angle with 90 degrees. Each of the other two angles are 45 degrees. The two sides opposite the smaller angles are equal in length.

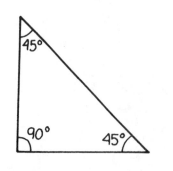

4. Examine the shapes. Find the five pieces which have the same shape as an isosceles right triangle.

5. The small square is easy to recognize. The last piece is a parallelogram. It has two 45 degree angles and two 135 degree angles.

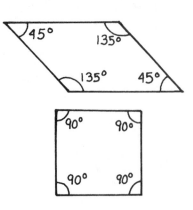

6. Use all of the shapes to make seven or more designs of your own. After each design is finished, outline the design on a piece of drawing paper. Give each design a name.

7. Without overlapping or leaving out any pieces, make the tightest design that you can. The tightest design would have the shortest distance around the pieces.

8. Measure the distance around the figure. Outline the figure on drawing paper.

Further Investigations

Tangram Teasers

1. Examine the seven pieces of your tangram. Arrange the two smallest triangles into a square. Arrange the two largest pieces into a square.

2. Arrange the two smallest triangles and the parallelogram into an isosceles right triangle.

3. Arrange the parallelogram, the two smallest triangles, and one of the largest triangles into a square.

4. Arrange the two largest triangles into a parallelogram.

5. Arrange the two smallest triangles, the one medium-sized triangle, and the square into a rectangle.

6. Arrange the square and the two smallest triangles into a trapezoid.

7. There are designs illustrated on page 89. Create each design by arranging your tangrams and outlining the arrangement of tangrams on your drawing paper.

Extension

Use a double set of tangrams on page 89 to make the three shapes shown on the bottom of the page. Research the story of tangrams and write stories to accompany your new designs.

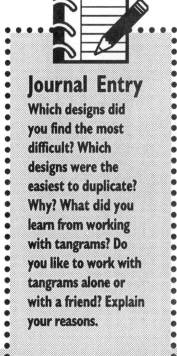

Journal Entry

Which designs did you find the most difficult? Which designs were the easiest to duplicate? Why? What did you learn from working with tangrams? Do you like to work with tangrams alone or with a friend? Explain your reasons.

Rubber Band Geometry

Individual/Partner Activity

Concepts

Geoboards, geometric shapes

Materials

Each team or student needs:

- reproducible, page 90
- scissors
- tape
- hammer
- 25 nails
- wooden blocks (6" x 6")
- thin rubber bands
- graph paper
- pencil

Rubber Band Geometry

1. Cut out the model for the geoboard on page 90. Tape it over one side of the wooden block.

2. Use a hammer to drive the nails securely into the wood at the 25 indicated points on the model.

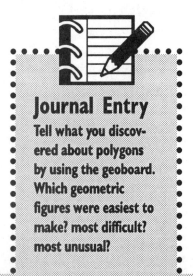

Journal Entry

Tell what you discovered about polygons by using the geoboard. Which geometric figures were easiest to make? most difficult? most unusual?

3. Use rubber bands to make as many squares as you can of different sizes on the geoboard. The rubber bands may overlap. Use graph paper to record the pattern of squares you find.

4. A polygon is a closed figure with three or more sides. Use the rubber bands to create as many different polygons as you can. Use graph paper to keep a record of each polygon you make. Try to create some polygons with five, six, seven, and eight sides.

5. Make as many different kinds of triangles as you can on your geoboard. Keep a record of each one on your paper.

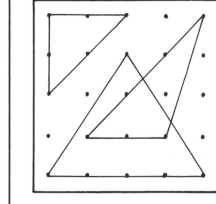

Further Investigations

Rubber Band Geometry

1. Create as many quadrilateral (four-sided) figures on the geoboard as you can. Keep a record on the drawing paper of the ones you make. Try to make several different sizes.

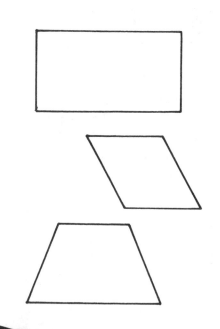

2. Some shapes are symmetrical and a line of symmetry can be drawn directly through the figure dividing it into two equal parts directly opposite each other. Use a rubber band to divide as many quadrilaterals as you can into two symmetrical parts.

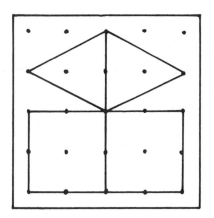

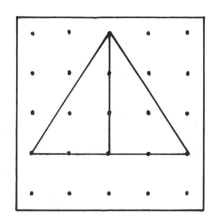

3. Create as many other shapes as you can which can be divided symmetrically. Try hexagons, triangles, and other figures. Keep a record of these on your drawing paper.

Extension

Measure the area of some of the shapes you have made. What are the smallest and largest areas possible of any given square, triangle, hexagon, and so forth? Use the geoboard to create designs of many different objects such as buildings, planes, rockets, and other artistic forms. How would you determine the area of these irregular figures?

Journal Entry

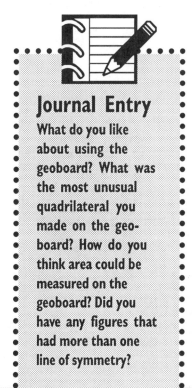

What do you like about using the geoboard? What was the most unusual quadrilateral you made on the geoboard? How do you think area could be measured on the geoboard? Did you have any figures that had more than one line of symmetry?

Napier's Bones

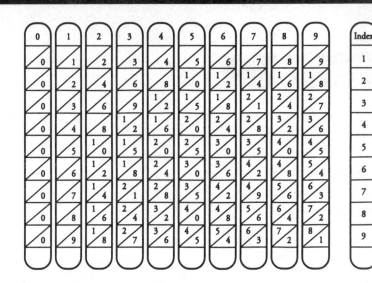

Concept

Napier's Bones, multiplication

Materials

Each student needs:

- 11 tongue depressors
- ruler
- colored pencils
- pencil
- reproducible, page 91
- masking tape
- writing paper

Napier's Bones

1. Study the illustration above. Line up your tongue depressors ("bones") and tape them together with masking tape.

2. Carefully measure from the top and mark every half inch on the first and last sticks. Use a ruler to draw ten straight lines directly through each half-inch marking. These lines must be measured and marked accurately.

3. Draw diagonal lines on the first ten tongue depressors as shown in the main illustration.

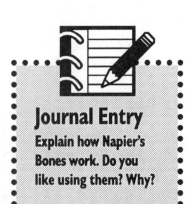

Journal Entry

Explain how Napier's Bones work. Do you like using them? Why?

4. Write the digits 0 through 9 on the top of the first 10 tongue depressors in a bright color. Write Index on the top of the last stick.

5. Write the digits 1 through 9 under the Index title in the same color you used for the digits on top of each tongue depressor.

6. Use a different color to fill in the multiplication table for each numbered stick.

7. Lay the tongue depressors down on a table with 8 and 2 next to each other. Place the Index next to these sticks.

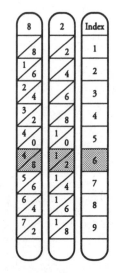

8. To multiply 82 times 6, look across from the 6 and write 492. You get the 9 by adding the numbers in the diagonal box, the parallelogram (8 + 1 = 9).

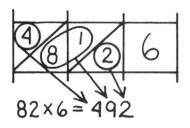

$$82 \times 6 = 492$$

9. Multiply 82 by each digit on the Index from 1 to 9 and record the answers on a separate sheet.

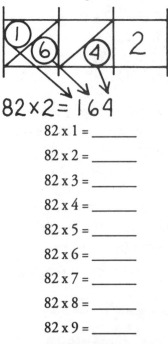

$$82 \times 2 = 164$$

82 x 1 = _____

82 x 2 = _____

82 x 3 = _____

82 x 4 = _____

82 x 5 = _____

82 x 6 = _____

82 x 7 = _____

82 x 8 = _____

82 x 9 = _____

Further Investigations

Make Some Bones About Math

1. Place the sticks numbered 4 and 5 next to each other. Place the Index to the right of them. Multiply 45 times each number on the Index and record the answers in the second column. Remember to add the digits in the diagonal box.

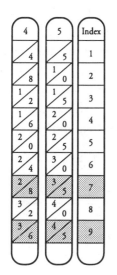

2. In the illustration below, when you get to the number 7 times 45, you have to carry a ten and rename. The answer is 315. In 9 times 45, you carry a ten again and the answer is 405. Study the illustration.

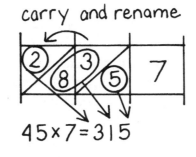

carry and rename

$45 \times 7 = 315$

carry and rename

$45 \times 9 = 405$

45 x 1 = _____

45 x 2 = _____

45 x 3 = _____

45 x 4 = _____

45 x 5 = _____

45 x 6 = _____

45 x 7 = _____

45 x 8 = _____

45 x 9 = _____

3. Practice with your Napier's Bones by doing these problems. Multiply each of the following numbers by all of the numbers on the Index. Record your answers on a chart.

95   54   83   68   59

4. Refer to page 91 for additional guidance and practice with Napier's Bones.

Extension

Who was Napier? Why did he invent these "bones"? How would you multiply longer numbers and two-digit multipliers with Napier's Bones? Use the "bones" to multiply these three-digit numbers by the Index.

843   364   647   736   385

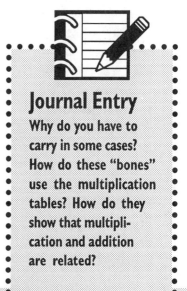

Journal Entry

Why do you have to carry in some cases? How do these "bones" use the multiplication tables? How do they show that multiplication and addition are related?

A Fibonacci in Time

Individual/Partner Activity

Concept

Sequences

Materials

Each student or team needs:
- calculator
- paper
- pencil

A Fibonacci in Time

1. Study the sequence of numbers shown here. Look for the pattern. Write in the missing numbers.

   (2, 4, 6, _____, 10, _____, 14,

   _____, _____, _____, _____)

2. Study the next sequence and determine what two operations were applied to each number in the sequence to obtain the next number. Fill in the missing numbers.

   (3, 7, 15, 31, _____, 127,

   _____, _____, _____, _____)

3. The next sequence is probably the most famous sequence in math. It is called the Fibonacci sequence, named for its 12th century discoverer. Find what has been done to obtain each term in the sequence. Fill in the missing numbers.

   (1, 1, 2, 3, 5, 8, 13, 21, _____,

   55, _____, _____, _____,

   _____)

4. Create your own number sequences with a hidden rule for each. Invite your classmates to complete each sequence and describe the mathematical rule.

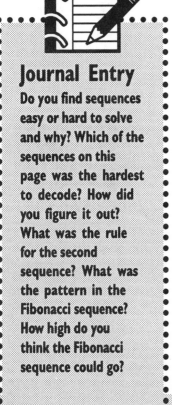

Journal Entry

Do you find sequences easy or hard to solve and why? Which of the sequences on this page was the hardest to decode? How did you figure it out? What was the rule for the second sequence? What was the pattern in the Fibonacci sequence? How high do you think the Fibonacci sequence could go?

Further Investigations

A Fibonacci in Time

1. Study the sequence written below. Find the pattern and fill in the missing numbers.

   (1, 4, 9, 16, 25, _____, 49,

   _____, _____, _____, _____,

   _____, _____)

2. Determine the rule of the following number sequence. Fill in the missing numbers.

   (2, 5, 10, 17, 26, _____, _____,

   _____, _____, _____, _____,

   _____, _____)

3. The following is an example of the Fibonacci sequence. Determine the rule and use your calculator to extend the Fibonacci sequence to 20 terms.

   (1, 1, 2, 3, 5, 8, 13, 21, 34, 55,

   _____, _____, _____, _____,

   _____, _____, _____, _____,

   _____, _____)

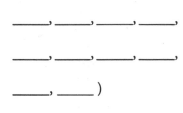

4. Find the missing numbers in the sequence below by using a Fibonacci-like method.

   (5, 7, 12, 19, 31, _____, _____,

   131, _____, _____, _____)

5. Create five other sequences and exchange your sequences with a classmate to solve.

Fibonacci Finds

1. Add the first ten numbers in the Fibonacci sequence. Check your answer by multiplying the seventh term (13) by 11. They should be the same answer.

2. Create your own Fibonacci-like sequence. Start with any two numbers and add them. Continue the sequence for ten terms. Add the ten terms. Multiply your seventh term by 11. You should obtain identical numbers.

Extension

How do you think the Fibonacci sequence or any sequence might be used to solve problems in math? Can you think of any sequences which you follow in your daily life?

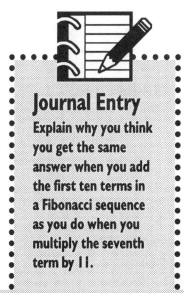

Journal Entry

Explain why you think you get the same answer when you add the first ten terms in a Fibonacci sequence as you do when you multiply the seventh term by 11.

Function Beans

Individual/Partner
Activity

Concepts

Patterns and functions

Materials

Each student or team needs:
- a small cup of beans
- 3 index cards
- calculator
- pencil

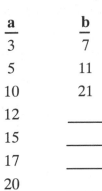

Function Beans

1. Study the function framework shown here to see what was done to "a" to get "b". It must be the same function each time.

a	b
3	7
5	11
10	21
12	___
15	___
17	___
20	___

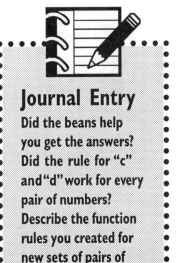

Journal Entry

Did the beans help you get the answers? Did the rule for "c" and "d" work for every pair of numbers? Describe the function rules you created for new sets of pairs of numbers in step 8.

2. Use an index card to make a title called "a". Use another index card for the title "b". Use a third index card titled "The Rule".

3. Arrange three beans on the "a" card. Arrange seven beans on the "b" card. Decide what operation or combination of operations could be used to get from three beans to seven beans.

4. After you have determined the hidden operation(s), apply the operation(s) to each pair of numbers ("a" and "b") to see if it consistently works. If it doesn't consistently work, try another operation or combination of operations until it consistently works for each pair of numbers.

5. If you tried "plus four," you found it worked on the first pair of numbers, but not on the next. Did you consider if multiplying the beans times 2 and adding 1 works each time?

6. On the Rule index card, write b = 2a + 1. Use the rule to find the missing number in column b. Use the beans to check each answer.

7. Use the beans and the three cards to determine the rule for "c" and "d" in this second function.

c	d
4	10
5	12
8	___
11	24
15	___
21	___
31	___

8. Create more charts of pairs of numbers. Determine the function and have a friend try to figure out the function.

Further Investigations

Function Beans

1. Use the beans to solve the two functions shown here. Try adding, multiplying by specific numbers, multiplying and adding, and multiplying and subtracting. Look for the rule which works every time with that function.

Function One		Function Two	
e	f	g	h
9	25	4	20
11	31	5	___
14	___	6	28
16	46	7	___
20	___	8	___
25	___	9	___
30	___	10	44

2. Use the beans to find the rule which works with each of these functions. Keep a record of each rule which did not work until you find the one which always fits.

Function Three		Function Four	
i	j	k	l
3	9	3	___
4	16	4	19
5	___	5	28
6	36	6	___
7	___	7	___
8	___	8	67
9	___	9	___
10	___	10	___

3. Use the beans to create four of your own function patterns like those you did on this page. Make sure that each function you make follows the rule for all numbers within the function.

4. Trade your functions with a friend and try to solve each other's functions using the beans to find the rules for each function.

5. Use your beans to create a function pattern using two or more operations. Challenge your friends to solve the functions.

Extension

Describe how functions might be used in everyday living. Illustrate your examples.

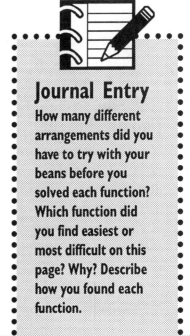

Journal Entry

How many different arrangements did you have to try with your beans before you solved each function? Which function did you find easiest or most difficult on this page? Why? Describe how you found each function.

Partner Activity

Concepts

Ratios, measurement

Materials

Each pair of students needs:
- 2 meter sticks
- calculator
- broomstick, mop, or pole
- chalk
- measuring tape (optional)

The Shadow Knows

1. Hold a meter stick directly upright in a sunny area of the playground near a short pole such as a broomstick, mop pole, or some other similar object.

2. Use chalk to mark the beginning and end of the shadow. Use another meter stick or a measuring tape to measure the length of the shadow created by the vertical meter stick.

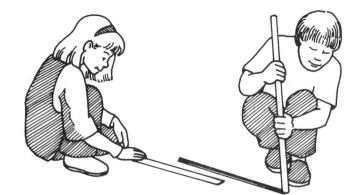

3. Measure the shadow projected by the pole in the same way.

4. Measure the shadow to the nearest centimeter so that 1 meter and 35 centimeters is 1.35 meters. In the same way, 85 centimeters is 0.85 meters.

5. Record your information on a chart like this one.

	Height of Object	Length of Shadow
Meter Stick	1 meter	_____
Pole	_____	_____

6. Multiply the height of the meter stick times the length of the pole's shadow.

7. Divide the answer by the length of the meter stick's shadow.

8. Use the measuring tape or meter stick to measure the actual length of the pole to see if your calculations were correct.

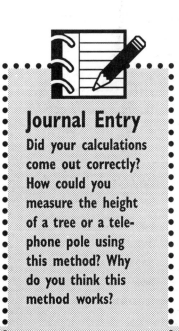

Journal Entry

Did your calculations come out correctly? How could you measure the height of a tree or a telephone pole using this method? Why do you think this method works?

Further Investigations

The Shadow Knows

1. Find a tetherball pole or another relatively short playground pole. Measure its shadow. Measure the shadow projected by your meter stick.

2. Multiply the height of your meter stick (1 meter) times the length of the pole's shadow.

3. Divide this answer by the length of the shadow cast by the meter stick.

4. Measure the height of the pole to see if your calculations were correct.

5. Use the same procedure for measuring the height of a tree on the playground. Use a chart like this one to record the information.

	Height of Object	Length of Shadow
Meter Stick	1 meter	_____
Tree	_____	_____

6. Now try some other objects. Use the method you learned to calculate the heights of the objects listed below. Use the chart to record your findings.

	Height of Object	Length of Shadow
Meter Stick	1 meter	_____
School	_____	_____
Flag Pole	_____	_____
Ball Wall	_____	_____
Basketball Pole	_____	_____
Second Tree	_____	_____
Playground Apparatus	_____	_____

Shadow Rule

$$\frac{\text{height of meter stick} \times \text{length of objects' shadow}}{\text{length of meter sticks' shadow}} = \text{height of object}$$

Extension

Would this system work on a cloudy day? Would the method work well at noon? Explain your reasons. What times of day would be most effective?

Journal Entry

Explain how "The Shadow Knows" technique for measurement works. Do your calculations seem reasonable?

Crayon Combos

Individual/Partner Activity

Concepts

Combinations, patterns

Materials

Each student or team needs:

- box of 12 crayons
- reproducible, page 92 (optional)

Crayon Combos

1. Select four of the colors from your box of crayons: red, green, blue, and yellow. Determine how many different color combinations you can make using these four colors. Remember that red/green is the same combination as green/red. A chart has been started for you. Complete the chart to determine the number of combinations.

Red/Green	Green/Blue	Blue/_____
Red/Blue	Green/_____	
Red/_____		

2. Use eight crayon colors (red, green, blue, yellow, brown, purple, black, orange) to determine how many different color combinations you could make using only two of the crayons at a time. Make a chart beginning like the one shown here indicating the possible different combinations.

Red/Green   Green/Blue
Red/Blue   Green/Yellow
Red/Yellow   Green/_____
Red/Brown   _____
Red/Purple   _____
Red/Black   _____
Red/Orange

Blue/Yellow   Yellow/Brown
Blue/_____   _____
_____   _____
_____   _____
_____

Brown/Purple   Purple/Black
_____   _____
_____

Black/_____

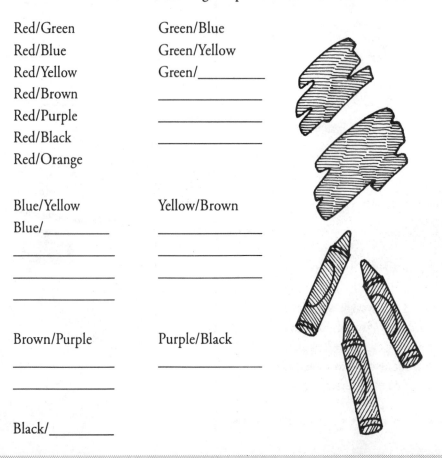

Journal Entry

How many different combinations did you get in steps 1 and 4? How does changing the number of available colors affect the outcome? Describe any mathematical patterns you noticed. Describe how you determined the number of combinations.

• Further Investigations

Crayon Combos

1. Choose five crayons such as red, green, blue, yellow, and orange to determine how many combinations you could make using only three of the five color choices.

2. Make a chart in the box to the right to show the pattern of combinations.

3. Use eight crayons to determine how many different pictures you can make using only three of the available eight colors for each picture. Use the chart on page 92 to record these color combinations.

Color Combination Chart

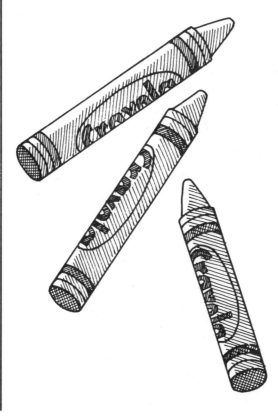

Extension

You have eight different schoolbooks at home. You can only bring three books to school on any day. Make a chart to help you determine how many different combinations of books you could carry to school.

Journal Entry

Why did the number of color combination possibilities decrease each time you started with a new color? What number pattern could you find for the combinations as you went from the first to the last set? Why do you think that using the eight crayons was much more complicated than five crayons?

Individual/Partner Activity

Concept

Patterns, sequences

Materials

Each student or team needs:

- reproducible, page 93
- calculator
- drawing paper
- tape
- pencil
- colored pencil
- ruler

Pascal's Triangle

1. Study the pattern shown in the triangular shape. Try to discover the pattern and fill in the missing numbers.

```
                          1
                       1     1
                    1     2     1
                 1     3     3     1
              1     4     6     4     1
           1     5    ___   ___   ___         1
        1     6    15    20    ___   ___   ___
     1     7    ___   35    ___   21     7    ___
  ___    8    28    56    70    ___   ___         1
1     9    ___   ___   ___        126    84    36    ___   ___
___   45   120   210   252   ___   ___   ___         10     1
```

Journal Entry

What pattern did you find in the totals? Study the triangle and find some other patterns which show a relationship between numbers above and below any given line. Describe the pattern. Where is the largest number in any line? How do you think this triangle might be used?

2. After filling in the missing spaces, check your work by comparing it to page 93. Notice the patterns.

3. Add each horizontal line of numbers and record a total for that line in the Line Total column on page 93.

Further Investigations

Pascal's Triangle

1. Use a pencil to draw upside-down triangles throughout the Pascal's Triangle on page 93. The bottom point of each triangle should point to the sum of the two numbers on the upper points of the triangle. The first two triangles are done for you in this illustration.

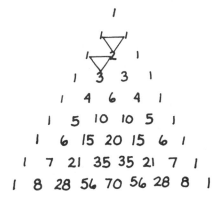

2. Tape a large sheet of drawing paper to the bottom of page 93. Extend the triangle for five more rows.. Use your calculator to compute the totals for each row.

3. Use your ruler and a colored pencil to draw lines like those shown in the illustration below for all the rows of Pascal's Triangle that you now have.

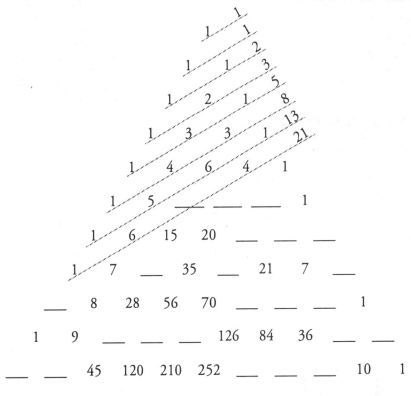

4. Add the totals for each diagonal. Study the totals. Notice any patterns.

Extension

Use your calculator to determine the totals for the next five lines without filling in any more of the triangle. What is the pattern? What will be the number to the right of the 1 on the 40th line? (The top 1 is considered line 0.) How could you use this triangle in a problem-solving situation? Write a problem that might be solved using Pascal's Triangle.

Did you see the pattern in the diagonal totals?

Journal Entry

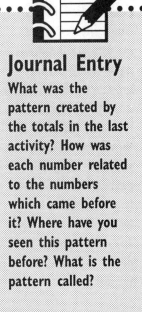

What was the pattern created by the totals in the last activity? How was each number related to the numbers which came before it? Where have you seen this pattern before? What is the pattern called?

Mighty Mobius

Individual Activity

Concept

Topology

Materials

Each student needs:

- several 18" to 24" long strips of paper, 1" wide
- pencil
- clear tape
- scissors

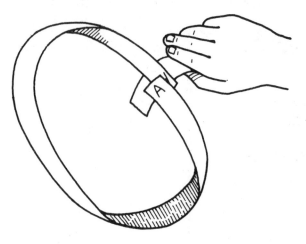

Mighty Mobius

1. Use a strip of paper about 18 inches long and 1 inch wide for this activity. Letter each end A as shown in the diagram.

2. Twist the strip once so that the two A's are overlapping. Tape the strip securely in this position. Make sure the tape covers the entire width of the strip.

Journal Entry

Describe what happened when you cut the strip. A Mobius strip is a continuous path like your first loop. Was the second strip a Mobius strip? How can you test it? What was different about the second path? Why do you think a Mobius strip works the way it does? Can you think of any possible uses for such a strip?

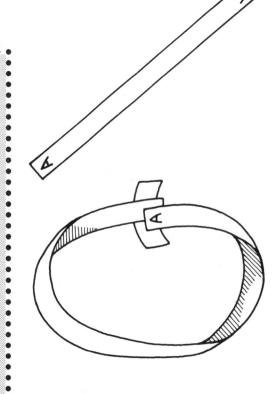

3. Use a pencil to draw a line along the center of the strip. Do not lift the pencil from the strip. Do not stop until you reach your starting point. What happened?

4. Use scissors to cut along the line you traced.

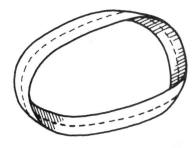

5. Examine the piece you have after cutting. Use a pencil to trace a path along the center of this strip. How does this path compare to the first one you drew?

Further Investigations

Mighty Mobius

1. Use a strip of paper 18 to 24 inches long and 2 inches wide for this activity. Label each end A as you did on the first page. Twist one end of the paper over and place A over A.

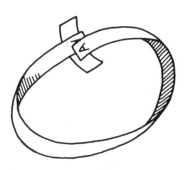

2. Tape the ends together on both sides. Make sure the tape covers the entire width of the strip. Draw a pencil path down the center of the strip until you reach your starting place.

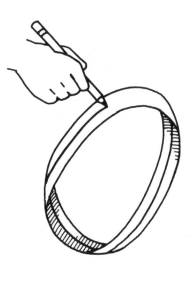

3. Cut the Mobius strip down the center as you did with the first one.

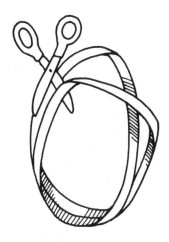

4. Trace a path down the center of the long loop as you did on the last page. Cut again along this new line.

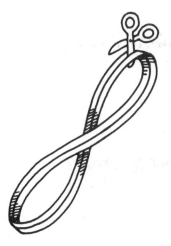

5. Examine the two intertwined loops. Do you think either or both could be a Mobius strip?

6. Use a pencil to trace a path along each loop.

Extension

Design a paper Mobius strip to accompany a classroom invention such as a continuous or repeating animated drawing, a belt to turn an automatic dispenser, or some similar device.

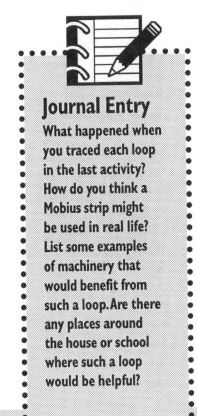

Journal Entry

What happened when you traced each loop in the last activity? How do you think a Mobius strip might be used in real life? List some examples of machinery that would benefit from such a loop. Are there any places around the house or school where such a loop would be helpful?

Card Sharp

Individual/Partner Activity

Concept

Probability, combinations

Materials

Each student or team needs:
● a deck of cards
● pencil

Card Sharp

1. Use a complete deck of 52 cards for this activity. Remove the Jokers.

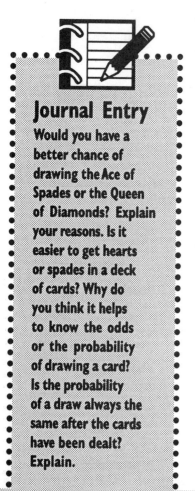

Journal Entry

Would you have a better chance of drawing the Ace of Spades or the Queen of Diamonds? Explain your reasons. Is it easier to get hearts or spades in a deck of cards? Why do you think it helps to know the odds or the probability of drawing a card? Is the probability of a draw always the same after the cards have been dealt? Explain.

2. Divide your deck into four piles: spades, hearts, clubs, and diamonds. You should have 13 cards in each pile.

3. Each pile should have an Ace, King, Queen, Jack and nine number cards (2 through 10).

4. Shuffle the deck and place it face down. Determine the probability of drawing each of the following cards.

Any Spade	13 in 52 or 1 in 4
Any Club	_____
Any Heart	_____
Any Diamond	_____
Any Ace	4 in 52 or 1 in 13
Any Queen	_____
King of Spades	_____
Queen of Hearts	_____
A Red Jack	_____
A Black 10	_____
Jack of Diamonds	_____
Any Red Card	_____
Any Black Card	_____
Any 2 or 3	_____
Any Face Card	_____
Any Number Card	_____

Further Investigations

Card Sharp

1. Use the following information to find all of the possible combinations of cards worth 10 points.

   Each Face Card (King, Queen, Jack) = 10 points

   Each Number Card = their face value (a 2 is worth 2 points, a 3 is worth 3 points, and so forth)

   An Ace may equal 1 or 11

2. Use the cards to determine the possible combinations that equal 10. You may combine as many cards as you wish to get 10 points. Make a chart like the one started here to illustrate the possible combinations. Remember, A=Ace, K=King, Q=Queen, J=Jacks, S=Spades, C=Clubs, H=Hearts, and D=Diamonds.

K of S	Q of S	J of S	10 of S
K of C	Q of C	_____	_____
K of H	_____	_____	_____
K of D	_____	_____	_____

A of S + 9 of C	A of S + 9 of H	A of S + 9 of S
A of C + 9 of C	A of C + 9 of H	_____
A of H + 9 of C	_____	_____
A of D + 9 of C	_____	_____

A of S + 9 of D	8 of S + 2 of C	8 of S + 2 of S
_____	8 of C + 2 of C	_____
_____	_____	_____
_____	_____	_____

and so on.

Extension

Use your cards to determine all the possible ways to make 21. Record your answers on a chart similar to the one on this page. Why do you think there are so many ways to make 21? Do you think there may be some that you missed?

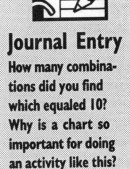

Journal Entry

How many combinations did you find which equaled 10? Why is a chart so important for doing an activity like this?

Pounding Pulses

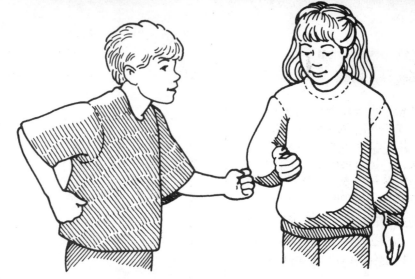

Partner Activity

Concepts

Measurement, estimation, averages

Materials

Each team needs:

● watch with second hand
● pencil
● paper
● calculator

Pounding Pulses

1. Hold your partner's left hand with your left hand. Place the index and middle finger of your right hand on the inside of the wrist as shown in the illustration.

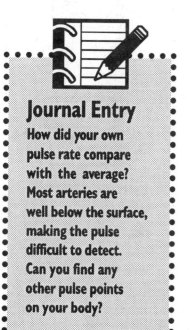

Journal Entry

How did your own pulse rate compare with the average? Most arteries are well below the surface, making the pulse difficult to detect. Can you find any other pulse points on your body?

2. Feel for your partner's pulse. The pulse is the contraction of the left ventricle of the heart as it pumps the blood from the heart through the arteries to the body.

3. Once you are certain you have found the pulse, count the number of beats in one minute. Record your count.

4. Have your partner find your pulse and record the number of beats in one minute.

5. Gather the results of eight more of your classmates and record the results on the chart below.

Resting Pulse Count in 1 Minute				
You	Partner	#3	#4	#5
___	___	___	___	___
#6	#7	#8	#9	#10
___	___	___	___	___

6. Average all the pulse readings. What was your average? Compare your average with those gathered by other students.

Further Investigations

Pounding Pulses

1. You and your partner should run in place, jog the track for one lap, do jumping jacks, jump rope, or do calisthenics for at least five minutes.

2. Immediately after exercising, take your own pulse for one minute. Record your results.

Extension

How are averages, medians, modes, and ranges useful? In what situations might the median or mode be the preferred average over the mean? Make a chart of all the males' resting pulse rates and a separate one for the females' resting pulse rates in your class. Observe the results. What conclusions might you draw?

3. Complete a chart, recording the pulse readings for yourself, your partner, and eight other classmates who have exercised in a similar manner.

Pulse Readings After Exercise

You	Partner	#3	#4	#5
____	____	____	____	____
#6	#7	#8	#9	#10
____	____	____	____	____

4. Average the results. Complete this table using the information on your chart.

Mean (add the scores and divide by 10) _____

Range (the difference between the lowest and highest reading) _____

Median (the reading closest to the middle) _____

Mode (the most often recorded reading) _____

5. Mean, median, and mode are types of statistical averages. Which do you think is most useful for this problem—mean, median, or mode? Why?

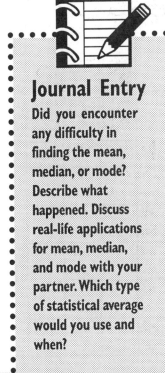

Journal Entry

Did you encounter any difficulty in finding the mean, median, or mode? Describe what happened. Discuss real-life applications for mean, median, and mode with your partner. Which type of statistical average would you use and when?

Footsies

Directions: Use the graph paper to outline your foot and your hand as instructed on the activity sheet, page 8–9.

Perimeter Pennies

Directions: Use figures A, B, and C with page 20–21.

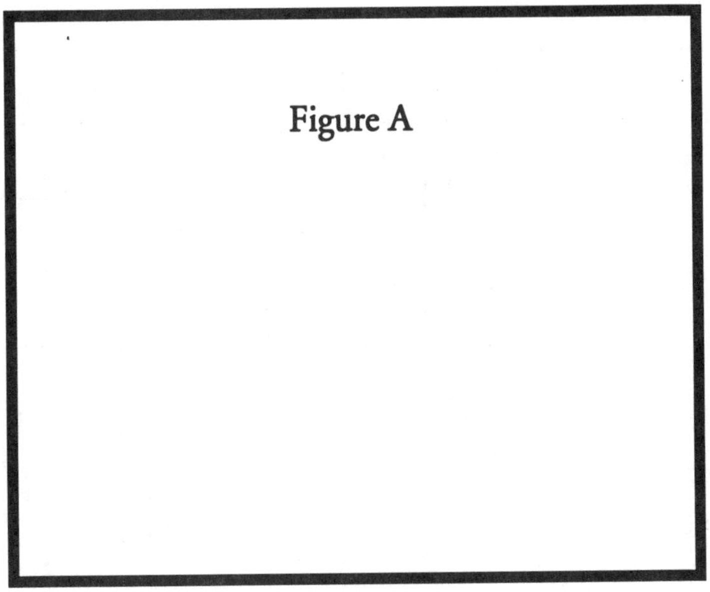

Figure A

Figure C

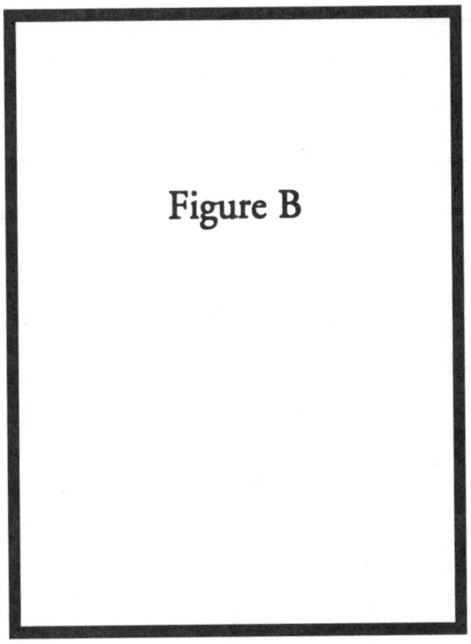

Figure B

Challenge: How would you compute the area and perimeter of Figure D?

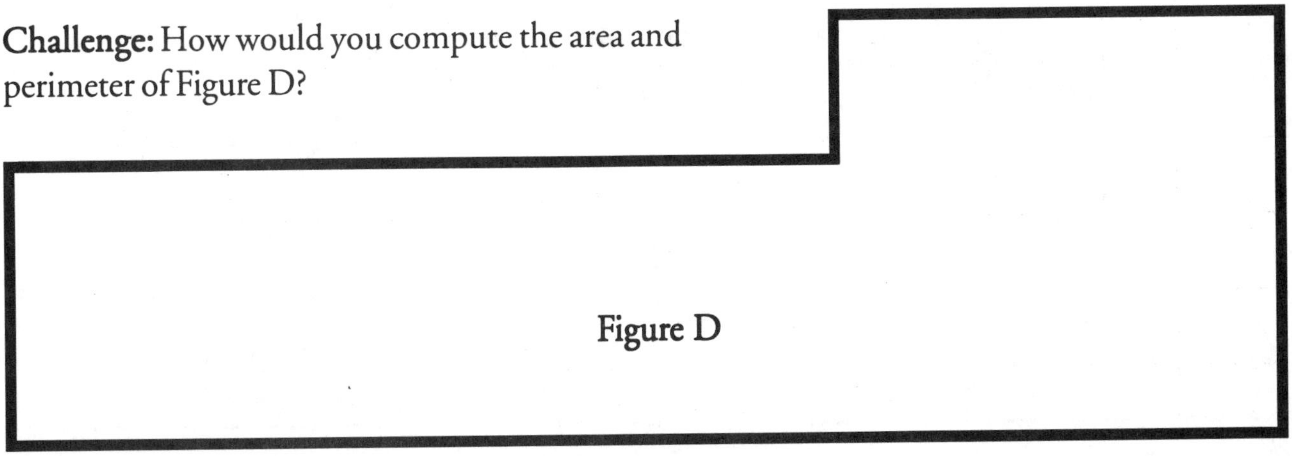

Figure D

Trophy Troubles

Directions: Cut out these trophies to use with the Trophy Troubles activity worksheets on pages 32–33.

This Trophy
Awarded
to

_____

**Most Considerate
Student**

Grade _____
Miss Nicynice

This Trophy
Awarded
to

_____

Best Athlete

Grade _____
Coach Crushem

**Super Speller
Award**

Given to

_____

**Never Missed
a Word**

Grade _____

**Best Coiffure, Do,
Cut, and Style**

Given to

_____

**By
Hairs R Us Salon**

Grade _____

**Math Wizard Award
Given to**

_____

Grade _____

**Number Cruncher
Extraordinaire**

**Student of the Year
Awarded to**

_____

Grade _____

School _____

**Principal
Ms. Goodheart**

Creative Teaching Press/ *Hands-On Math for Middle Grades*

Prime Picks

Name _____

Directions: Use this page when you do the investigations on activity pages 34–35.

Circle all of the prime numbers between 2 and 100.

1	2	3	4	5	6	7	8	9	10
11	12	13	14	15	16	17	18	19	20
21	22	23	24	25	26	27	28	29	30
31	32	33	34	35	36	37	38	39	40
41	42	43	44	45	46	47	48	49	50
51	52	53	54	55	56	57	58	59	60
61	62	63	64	65	66	67	68	69	70
71	72	73	74	75	76	77	78	79	80
81	82	83	84	85	86	87	88	89	90
91	92	93	94	95	96	97	98	99	100

Circle all of the prime numbers between 101 and 200.

101	102	103	104	105	106	107	108	109	110
111	112	113	114	115	116	117	118	119	120
121	122	123	124	125	126	127	128	129	130
131	132	133	134	135	136	137	138	139	140
141	142	143	144	145	146	147	148	149	150
151	152	153	154	155	156	157	158	159	160
161	162	163	164	165	166	167	168	169	170
171	172	173	174	175	176	177	178	179	180
181	182	183	184	185	186	187	188	189	190
191	192	193	194	195	196	197	198	199	200

Use this chart to help you find the largest prime number less than 1000.

999	998	997	996	995	994	993	992	991	990
989	988	987	986	985	984	983	982	981	980
979	978	977	976	975	974	973	972	971	970
969	968	967	966	965	964	963	962	961	960
959	958	957	956	955	954	953	952	951	950
949	948	947	946	945	944	943	942	941	940
939	938	937	936	935	934	933	932	931	930
929	928	927	926	925	924	923	922	921	920
919	918	917	916	915	914	913	912	911	910
909	908	907	906	905	904	903	902	901	900

Challenge: Can you find all of the prime numbers in the chart above?

Toothpick Bases

Directions: Use your toothpicks to help you write the following examples in base three.

//   _____ (base three)   /// /// /   _____ (base three)

///   _____ (base three)   /// /// //   _____ (base three)

/// /   _____ (base three)   /// /// ///   _____ (base three)

/// //   _____ (base three)   /// /// /// /   _____ (base three)

/// ///   _____ (base three)   /// /// /// //   _____ (base three)

Base Three with Larger Numbers

Arrange your toothpicks in base three piles to write these larger numbers.

Base Ten Number	Toothpick Arrangement	Base Three Number
19	///////// ///////// /	201 (base three)
20	///////// ///////// //	_____ (base three)
21		_____ (base three)
25		_____ (base three)
27		1000 (base three)
28		1001 (base three)
29		_____ (base three)
36		_____ (base three)
37		_____ (base three)
40		_____ (base three)
41		_____ (base three)
45		_____ (base three)
46		_____ (base three)
54		_____ (base three)
55		_____ (base three)

Using Base Three with Higher Values

1. If you had 81 toothpicks, it would be written as 10,000 (base three). This is read as "1 eighty-one, no twenty-sevens, no nines, no threes, and no ones (base three)."

2. How would you write 2 eighty-ones, 2 twenty-sevens, 2 nines, 2 threes, and 2 ones?

   _____ (base three)

   What base ten number is this?

3. How many toothpicks would it take to represent 100,000 (base three)?

   _____

Flying Geometry

Directions: Use the examples shown here to help you construct the plane to be used for pages 42-43.

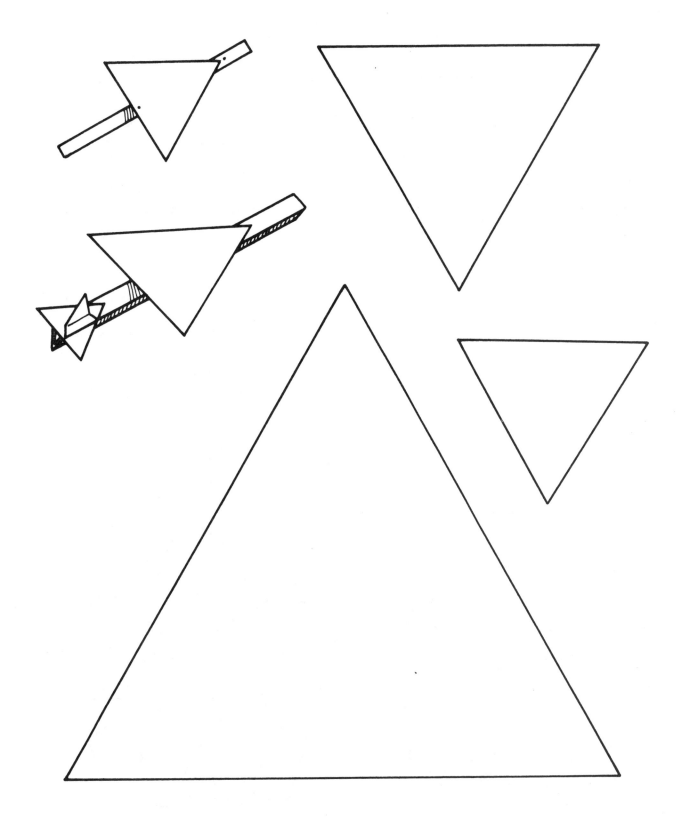

Dicey Dodecahedrons, Part 1

Directions: Use this page to accompany the Dicey Dodecahedrons activity sheets on pages 50–51.

Pentagon Models

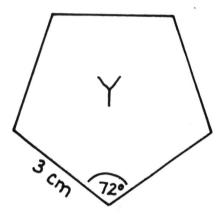 

Dodecahedral Die Model

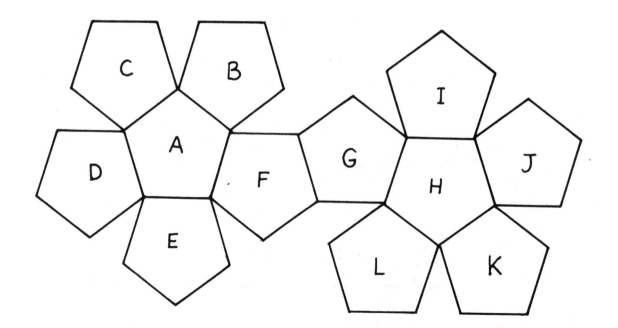

Dicey Dodecahedrons, Part II

Directions: Use this page to accompany the Dicey Dodecahedrons activity sheets on pages 50–51.

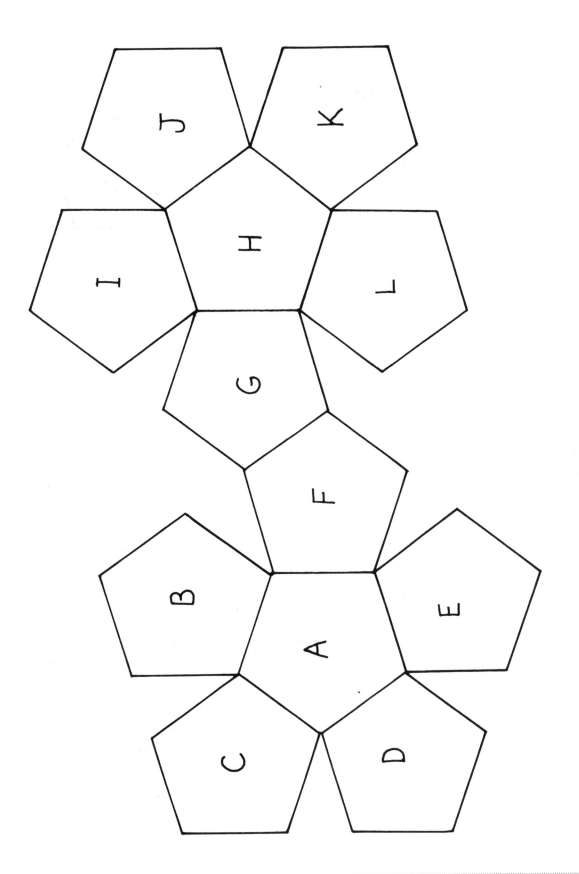

Heads Up

Name _____

Directions: Use this page to record results of activities from pages 52–53.

	Column One Penny Flips	Column Two 1 Die Roll	Column Three 2 Dice Roll	Column Four 3 Dice Roll		Column One Penny Flips	Column Two 1 Die Roll	Column Three 2 Dice Roll	Column Four 3 Dice Roll
1.					25.				
2.					26.				
3.					27.				
4.					28.				
5.					29.				
6.					30.				
7.					31.				
8.					32.				
9.					33.				
10.					34.				
11.					35.				
12.					36.				
13.					37.				
14.					38.				
15.					39.				
16.					40.				
17.					41.				
18.					42.				
19.					43.				
20.					44.				
21.					45.				
22.					46.				
23.					47.				
24.					48.				

Creative Teaching Press/ *Hands-On Math for Middle Grades*

Graphing Grid

Name_____

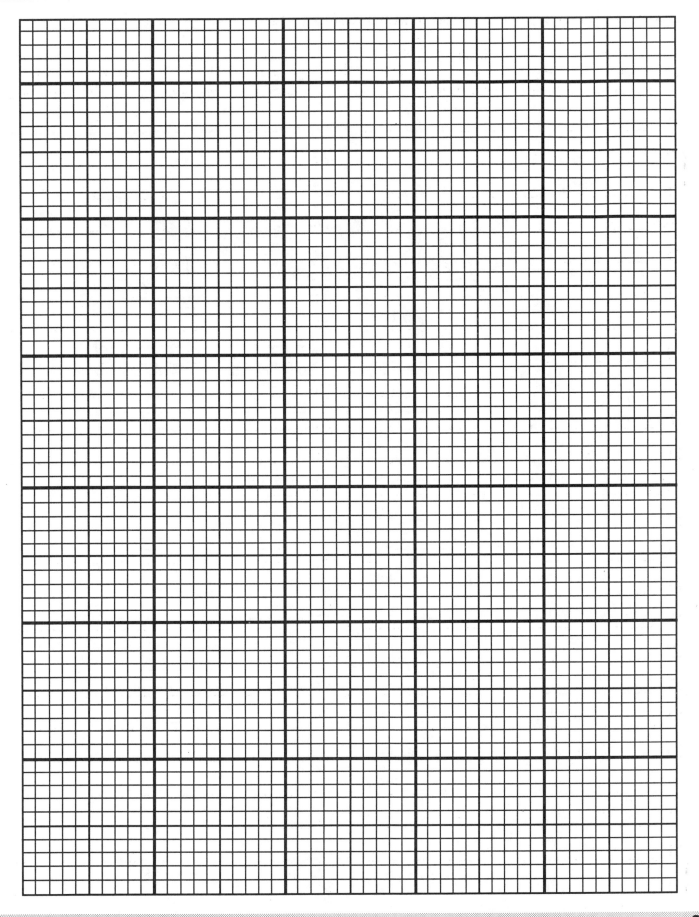

Buggy Math

Name _____

Directions: Use the chart below to record the results of your Buggy Math investigations on pages 54–55.

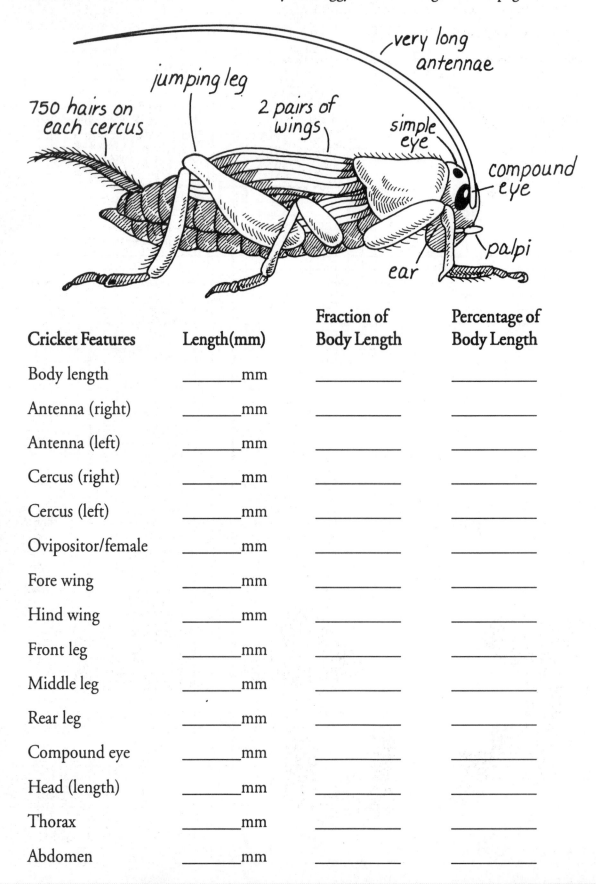

Cricket Features	Length(mm)	Fraction of Body Length	Percentage of Body Length
Body length	_____mm	_____	_____
Antenna (right)	_____mm	_____	_____
Antenna (left)	_____mm	_____	_____
Cercus (right)	_____mm	_____	_____
Cercus (left)	_____mm	_____	_____
Ovipositor/female	_____mm	_____	_____
Fore wing	_____mm	_____	_____
Hind wing	_____mm	_____	_____
Front leg	_____mm	_____	_____
Middle leg	_____mm	_____	_____
Rear leg	_____mm	_____	_____
Compound eye	_____mm	_____	_____
Head (length)	_____mm	_____	_____
Thorax	_____mm	_____	_____
Abdomen	_____mm	_____	_____

Creative Teaching Press/ *Hands-On Math for Middle Grades*

Tangram Teasers

1. Directions: Cut out these tangram pieces and use them as a model to cut pieces from heavy posterboard or cardboard. Keep your tangram pieces in a plastic bag.

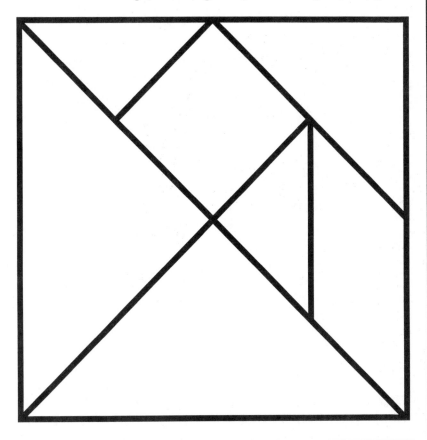

2. Directions: Arrange all of the pieces of the tangram to create the designs.

Olympic Flame

Hot Air Balloon

Angel at Rest

Bird

Rectangle

Bushy-Tailed Fox

3. Directions: Arrange all of the pieces of two sets of tangrams to make these two designs.

Hockey Goalie   **Kite**

To be used with pages 56–57.

Rubber Band Geometry

Directions: Cut out the square below. Tape this to your six-inch square board. Hammer a nail into each spot indicated to create your geoboard.

To be used with pages 58–59.

Creative Teaching Press/*Hands-On Math for Middle Grades*

Napier's Bones

Name _____

Directions: Study the problems below. Notice how the shaded circled areas show how to determine the appropriate digit for the tens place of the product.

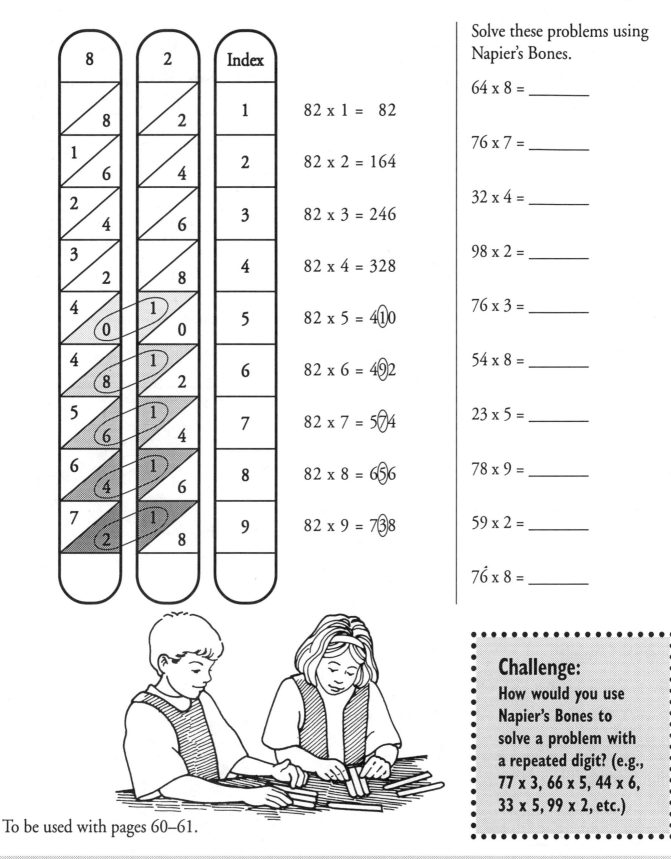

8	2	Index
		1
		2
		3
		4
		5
		6
		7
		8
		9

82 x 1 =   82

82 x 2 = 164

82 x 3 = 246

82 x 4 = 328

82 x 5 = 4⑴0

82 x 6 = 4⑼2

82 x 7 = 5⑺4

82 x 8 = 6⑸6

82 x 9 = 7⑶8

Solve these problems using Napier's Bones.

64 x 8 = _____

76 x 7 = _____

32 x 4 = _____

98 x 2 = _____

76 x 3 = _____

54 x 8 = _____

23 x 5 = _____

78 x 9 = _____

59 x 2 = _____

76 x 8 = _____

Challenge:
How would you use Napier's Bones to solve a problem with a repeated digit? (e.g., 77 x 3, 66 x 5, 44 x 6, 33 x 5, 99 x 2, etc.)

To be used with pages 60–61.

Crayon Combos

Name_____

Directions: Complete the chart to illustrate all of the different color combinations you can make using three colors from a box of eight crayons. The colors you need are red, green, blue, brown, yellow, orange, black, and purple.

Red/Green/Blue

Red/Green/Brown

Red/Green/Yellow

Red/Green/_____

Red/Green/_____

Red/Green/_____

Red/Yellow/Orange

Red/Yellow/_____

Red/_____/_____

Red/Blue/Brown

Red/Blue/_____

Red/_____/_____

_____/_____/_____

_____/_____/_____

Red/Brown/Yellow

Red/Brown/_____

_____/_____/_____

_____/_____/_____

Red/Orange/Black

Red/Orange/_____

Red/Black/_____

Green/Blue/Brown

Green/Blue/Yellow

Green/Blue/_____

Green/Blue/_____

Green/Blue/_____

Green/Orange/Black

_____/_____/_____

Green/Brown/Yellow

Green/Brown/Orange

Green/Brown/_____

_____/_____/_____

Green/Black/_____

Green/Yellow/Orange

Green/Yellow/_____

_____/_____/_____

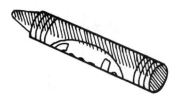

Blue/Brown/Yellow

Blue/Brown/Orange

Blue/_____/_____

_____/_____/_____

Blue/Black/Purple

Blue/Yellow/Orange

Blue/Yellow/_____

_____/_____/_____

Blue/Orange/Black

Blue/_____/_____

Brown/Yellow/Orange

Brown/Yellow/Black

Brown/Yellow/Purple

Yellow/Orange/Black

Yellow/Orange/_____

Orange/_____/_____

Brown/Orange/Black

Brown/Orange/_____

Yellow/Black/_____

Brown/_____/_____

To be used with pages 68–69.

Creative Teaching Press/ Hands-On Math for Middle Grades

Pascal's Triangle

Name _____

Directions: Fill in the missing blanks in Pascal's Triangle.
Add up the total for each line.

Pascal's Triangle

Line Totals

```
                    1                          _____

                 1     1                       _____

              1     2     1                    _____

           1     3     3     1                 _____

        1     4     6     4     1              _____

     1     5    10    10     5     1           _____

  1     6    15    20    15     6     1        _____

1     7    21    35    35    21     7     1    _____

1     8    28    56    70    56    28     8     1     _____

1     9    36    84   126   126    84    36     9     1     _____

1   10    45   120   210   252   210   120    45    10     1   _____
```

___ ___ ___ ___ ___ ___ ___ ___ ___ ___ ___

Directions: Go back and extend Pascal's Triangle by adding five more rows.

To be used with pages 70–71.

Answer Key

Pages that do not require specific answers have been omitted.

Page 13–More Rule of Six Fun

4. There are 6 interior angles in a hexagon.
   There are 12 interior angles in a dodecagon.
   Angles in a regular hexagon measure 120 degrees.
   Angles in a regular dodecagon measure 150 degrees.

Page 19

Figure	Faces	Edges	Vertices
Triangular Pyramid	4	6	4
Square Pyramid	5	8	5
Triangular Prism	5	9	6
Rectangular Prism	6	12	8
Cube	6	12	8
Octahedron	8	12	6

Page 20

2. P of Figure A = 18 pennies
3. P of Figure B = 14 pennies

Page 21

1. A of Figure C = 15 pennies
3. A of Figure A = 20 pennies
   A of Figure B = 12 pennies
4. Approximately 28 pennies

Page 22

1. 4   2. 9   3. 16
4. Chart

Pennies on One Side	Total Pennies in Square
2	4
3	9
4	16
5	25
6	36
7	49
8	64
9	81
10	100

5. Largest square with 3 rolls of pennies - 144
   Largest square with 4 rolls of pennies - 196
   Largest square with 5 rolls of pennies - 225
6. A square with 1,000 pennies on a side would use 1,000,000 pennies worth $10,000.

Page 23

1. $6 \times 6 = 6^2 = 36$
   $7 \times 7 = 7^2 = 49$
   $8 \times 8 = 8^2 = 64$
   $9 \times 9 = 9^2 = 81$

2. $12^2 = 144$
   $13^2 = 169$
   $14^2 = 196$
   $15^2 = 225$
   $16^2 = 256$
   $17^2 = 289$
   $18^2 = 324$
   $19^2 = 361$
   $20^2 = 400$
   $25^2 = 625$

Page 23–Square Roots

3.
Number	Square Root
25	5
81	9
100	10
121	11
144	12
169	13

4. The square root of 625 is 25.

Extension:
Number	Square Root
400	20
900	30
1600	40
2500	50
8100	90
6400	80
4900	70
3600	60
14,400	120
810,000	900
25,000,000	5000

Page 29

1.
Planet	100 lb. Person	250 lb. Person
Mercury	38 lb.	95 lb.
Venus	90 lb.	225 lb.
Earth	100 lb.	250 lb.
Mars	38 lb.	95 lb.
Jupiter	287 lb.	717.5 lb.
Saturn	132 lb.	330 lb.
Uranus	93 lb.	232.5 lb.
Neptune	123 lb.	307.5 lb.
Pluto	3 lb.	7.5 lb.

Page 30

3. 28,800 dollars counted in an 8 hr. day
   Dollars Per Year
2. 10,512,000 dollars counted in 1 year.

Page 31

1. 105,120,000 dollars counted in 10 years
3. 50 years - 525,600,000 dollars counted
   60 years - 630,720,000 dollars counted
   70 years - 735,840,000 dollars counted
   80 years - 840,960,000 dollars counted
   90 years - 946,080,000 dollars counted

Trillions and Quadrillions

1. It would take over 95 thousand years to count a trillion dollars and over 95 million years to count a quadrillion dollars.

Page 32

4.
MC	BA	SS
MC	SS	BA
BA	MC	SS
BA	SS	MC
SS	BA	MC
SS	MC	BA

6. 24 different arrangements

Page 33–Working With Factorials

2. $6 \times 5 \times 4 \times 3 \times 2 \times 1 = 720$
3. $7 \times 6 \times 5 \times 4 \times 3 \times 2 \times 1 = 5040$
   $8 \times 7 \times 6 \times 5 \times 4 \times 3 \times 2 \times 1 = 40,320$
   $9 \times 8 \times 7 \times 6 \times 5 \times 4 \times 3 \times 2 \times 1 = 362,880$
   $10 \times 9 \times 8 \times 7 \times 6 \times 5 \times 4 \times 3 \times 2 \times 1 = 3,628,800$

Page 34

10. Prime Numbers between 1 and 100 are: 2, 3, 5, 7, 11, 13, 17, 19, 23, 29, 31, 37, 41, 43, 47, 53, 59, 61, 67, 71, 73, 79, 83, 89, 97.

(2)	(3)	4	(5)	6	(7)	8	9	10
(11)	12	(13)	14	15	16	(17)	18	(19)	20
21	22	(23)	24	25	26	27	28	(29)	30
(31)	32	33	34	35	36	(37)	38	39	40
(41)	42	(43)	44	45	46	(47)	48	49	50
51	52	(53)	54	55	56	57	58	(59)	60
(61)	62	63	64	65	66	(67)	68	69	70
(71)	72	(73)	74	75	76	77	78	(79)	80
81	82	(83)	84	85	86	87	88	(89)	90
91	92	93	94	95	96	(97)	98	99	100

Page 35

1. Prime Numbers between 101 and 200 are: 101, 103, 107, 109, 113, 127, 131, 137, 139, 149, 151, 157, 163, 167, 173, 179, 181, 191, 193, 197, 199.

(101)	102	(103)	104	105	106	(107)	108	(109)	110
111	112	(113)	114	115	116	117	118	119	120
121	122	123	124	125	126	(127)	128	129	130
(131)	132	133	134	135	136	(137)	138	(139)	140
141	142	143	144	145	146	147	148	(149)	150
(151)	152	153	154	155	156	(157)	158	159	160
161	162	(163)	164	165	166	(167)	168	169	170
171	172	(173)	174	175	176	177	178	(179)	180
(181)	182	183	184	185	186	187	188	189	190
(191)	192	(193)	194	195	196	(197)	198	(199)	200

2. There are 21 Prime Numbers between 101 and 200.
4. 289 is the first multiple of 17 over 200.

Extension: The largest prime number under 1000 is 997.

Answer Key

Page 36

4.
Base 10	Base 3
7	21
8	22
9	100
10	101
11	102
12	110
27	1000
28	1001
30	1010
55	2001

Page 37

6.
Base Three Number	Toothpicks	Base Ten Number
121	16	16
122	17	17
222	26	26

7.
Base Ten	Base Three
29	$1002_{(base three)}$
31	$1011_{(base three)}$
36	$1100_{(base three)}$
38	$1102_{(base three)}$
44	$1122_{(base three)}$
55	$2001_{(base three)}$
64	$2101_{(base three)}$
1000	$1,101,001_{(base three)}$

Journal Entry 81

Page 38

4.
35	44	8	24	30
1 x 35	1 x 44	1 x 8	1 x 24	1 x 30
35 x 1	44 x 1	8 x 1	24 x 1	30 x 1
5 x 7	2 x 22	2 x 4	2 x 12	2 x 15
7 x 5	22 x 2	4 x 2	12 x 2	15 x 2
	4 x 11		3 x 8	3 x 10
	11 x 4		8 x 3	10 x 3
			4 x 6	5 x 6
			6 x 4	6 x 5

Page 39

1. Factor pairs for 36 are: 1 x 36, 36 x 1, 2 x 18, 18 x 2, 3 x 12, 12 x 3, 4 x 9, 9 x 4, 6 x 6.

2.
100	80	69	48	72
1 x 100	1 x 80	1 x 69	1 x 48	1 x 72
100 x 1	80 x 1	69 x 1	48 x 1	72 x 1
2 x 50	2 x 40	3 x 23	2 x 24	2 x 36
50 x 2	40 x 2	23 x 3	24 x 2	36 x 2
4 x 25	4 x 20		4 x 12	3 x 24
25 x 4	20 x 4		12 x 4	24 x 3
5 x 20	5 x 16		6 x 8	4 x 18
20 x 5	16 x 5		8 x 6	18 x 4
10 x 10	8 x 10			6 x 12
	10 x 8			12 x 6
				8 x 9
				9 x 8

55	88	96	360
1 x 55	1 x 88	1 x 96	1 x 360
55 x 1	88 x 1	96 x 1	360 x 1
5 x 11	2 x 44	2 x 48	2 x 180
11 x 5	44 x 2	48 x 2	180 x 2
	4 x 22	3 x 32	3 x 120
	22 x 4	32 x 3	120 x 3
	8 x 11	4 x 24	4 x 90
	11 x 8	24 x 4	90 x 4
		6 x 16	5 x 72
		16 x 6	72 x 5
		8 x 12	6 x 60
		12 x 8	60 x 6
			8 x 45
			45 x 8
			9 x 40
			40 x 9
			10 x 36
			36 x 10
			12 x 30

Page 39 (cont.)

360
30 x 12
15 x 24
24 x 15
18 x 20
20 x 18

4. The numbers in this section (19, 23, 11, 31, 41, 67, 97, 5, 17, and 29) are prime. The only factors are 1 and the number itself.

Page 41

Journal Entry

There are 4 equilateral triangular faces in the tetrahedron with 4 vertices and 6 edges.

Page 49

11. A cube has 6 faces, 12 edges, and 8 vertices.

Page 51

6.
	Tetrahedron	Octahedron	Cube	Dodecahedron
Faces	4	8	6	12
Edges	6	12	12	30
Vertices	4	6	8	20

Page 60

9.
82 x 1 = 82
82 x 2 = 164
82 x 3 = 246
82 x 4 = 328
82 x 5 = 410
82 x 6 = 492
82 x 7 = 574
82 x 8 = 656
82 x 9 = 738

Page 61

2.
45 x 1 = 45
45 x 2 = 90
45 x 3 = 135
45 x 4 = 180
45 x 5 = 225
45 x 6 = 270
45 x 7 = 315
45 x 8 = 360
45 x 9 = 405

Page 62

1. (2, 4, 6, 8, 10, 12, 14, 16, 18, 20, 22)
2. (3, 7, 15, 31, 63, 127, 255, 511, 1023, 2047)
3. (1, 1, 2, 3, 5, 8, 13, 21, 34, 55, 89, 144, 233, 377)

Page 63

1. (1, 4, 9, 16, 25, 36, 49, 64, 81, 100, 121, 144, 169)
2. (2, 5, 10, 17, 26, 37, 50, 65, 82, 101, 122, 145, 170)
3. (1, 1, 2, 3, 5, 8, 13, 21, 34, 55, 89, 144, 233, 377, 610, 987, 1597, 2584, 4181, 6765)
4. (5, 7, 12, 19, 31, 50, 81, 131, 212, 343, 555)

Fibonacci Finds

1. (143 is the answer)

Page 64

1. b = 7, 11, 21, 25, 31, 35, 41
7. d = 10, 12, 18, 24, 32, 44, 64   d = (c x 2) + 2

Page 65

1. f = 25, 31, 40, 46, 58, 73, 88   f = (e x 3) - 2
   h = 20, 24, 28, 32, 36, 40, 44   h = (g x 4) + 4
2. j = 9, 16, 25, 36, 49, 64, 81, 100   j = (i x i)
   l = 12, 19, 28, 39, 52, 67, 84, 103   l = (k x k) + 3

Answer Key

Page 68
1. Red/Green   Green/Blue   Blue/Yellow
   Red/Blue   Green/Yellow
   Red/Yellow

2. Red/Green   Green/Blue   Blue/Yellow   Yellow/Brown
   Red/Blue   Green/Yellow   Blue/Brown   Yellow/Purple
   Red/Yellow   Green/Brown   Blue/Purple   Yellow/Black
   Red/Brown   Green/Purple   Blue/Black   Yellow/Orange
   Red/Purple   Green/Black   Blue/Orange
   Red/Black   Green/Orange
   Red/Orange

   Brown/Purple   Purple/Black   Black/Orange
   Brown/Black   Purple/Orange
   Brown/Orange

Page 69
1. Red/Green/Blue   Red/Blue/Yellow   Red/Yellow/Orange
   Red/Green/Yellow   Red/Blue/Orange
   Red/Green/Orange

   Green/Blue/Yellow   Green/Yellow/Orange
   Green/Blue/Orange

   Blue/Yellow/Orange

Page 70
Answers on page 93

Page 71
Extension:
(40 will be to the right of 1 on the 40th line)

3. The numbers create the Fibonacci Sequence (1, 1, 2, 3, 5, 8, 13, 21, 34, 55, 89, 144, 233, 377, 610, 987, 1597)

Page 74

4. Any Spade	13 in 52 or 1 in 4
Any Club	13 in 52 or 1 in 4
Any Heart	13 in 52 or 1 in 4
Any Diamond	13 in 52 or 1 in 4
Any Ace	4 in 52 or 1 in 13
Any Queen	4 in 52 or 1 in 13
King of Spades	1 in 52
Queen of Hearts	1 in 52
Red Jack	2 in 52 or 1 in 26
Black 10	2 in 52 or 1 in 26
Jack of Diamonds	1 in 52
Any Red Card	26 in 52 or 1 in 2
Any Black Card	26 in 52 or 1 in 2
Any 2 or 3	8 in 52 or 2 in 13
Any Face Card	12 in 52 or 3 in 13
Any Number Card	36 in 52 or 9 in 13

Page 75
2. K of S   Q of S   J of S   10 of S
   K of C   Q of C   J of C   10 of C
   K of H   Q of H   J of H   10 of H
   K of D   Q of D   J of D   10 of D

   A of C + 9 of C   A of C + 9 of H   A of C + 9 of S
   A of H + 9 of C   A of H + 9 of H   A of H + 9 of S
   A of D + 9 of C   A of D + 9 of H   A of D + 9 of S

   A of S + 9 of D   8 of S + 2 of C   8 of S + 2 of S
   A of C + 9 of D   8 of C + 2 of C   8 of C + 2 of S
   A of H + 9 of D   8 of H + 2 of C   8 of H + 2 of S
   A of D + 9 of D   8 of D + 2 of C   8 of D + 2 of S
   and so on.

Page 81
Primes between 1–200 listed on page 94 of the Answer Key under pages 34–35.

Primes between 900–999 are: 907, 911, 919, 929, 937, 941, 947, 953, 967, 971, 977, 983, 991, 997.

Page 82

$2_{(\text{base three})}$ $21_{(\text{base three})}$
$10_{(\text{base three})}$ $22_{(\text{base three})}$
$11_{(\text{base three})}$ $100_{(\text{base three})}$
$12_{(\text{base three})}$ $101_{(\text{base three})}$
$20_{(\text{base three})}$ $102_{(\text{base three})}$

Base Ten	Toothpicks	Base Three Number
19	19	$201_{(\text{base three})}$
20	20	$202_{(\text{base three})}$
21	21	$210_{(\text{base three})}$
25	25	$221_{(\text{base three})}$
27	27	$1000_{(\text{base three})}$
28	28	$1001_{(\text{base three})}$
29	29	$1002_{(\text{base three})}$
36	36	$1100_{(\text{base three})}$

Base Ten	Toothpicks	Base Three Number
37	37	$1101_{(\text{base three})}$
40	40	$1111_{(\text{base three})}$
41	41	$1112_{(\text{base three})}$
45	45	$1200_{(\text{base three})}$
46	46	$1201_{(\text{base three})}$
54	54	$2000_{(\text{base three})}$
55	55	$2001_{(\text{base three})}$

2. $22222_{(\text{base three})} = 242_{(\text{base ten})}$
3. $100{,}000_{(\text{base three})} = 243_{(\text{base ten})}$

Page 91
64 x 8 = 512   76 x 7 = 532   32 x 4 = 128
98 x 2 = 196   76 x 3 = 228   54 x 8 = 432
23 x 5 = 115   78 x 9 = 702   59 x 2 = 118
76 x 8 = 608

Page 92

Red/Green/Blue   Red/Blue/Brown   Red/Brown/Yellow
Red/Green/Brown   Red/Blue/Yellow   Red/Brown/Orange
Red/Green/Yellow   Red/Blue/Orange   Red/Brown/Black
Red/Green/Orange   Red/Blue/Black   Red/Brown/Purple
Red/Green/Black   Red/Blue/Purple
Red/Green/Purple

Red/Yellow/Orange   Red/Orange/Black   Red/Black/Purple
Red/Yellow/Black   Red/Orange/Purple
Red/Yellow Purple

Green/Blue/Brown   Green/Brown/Yellow   Green/Yellow/Orange
Green/Blue/Yellow   Green/Brown/Orange   Green/Yellow/Black
Green/Blue/Orange   Green/Brown/Black   Green/Yellow/Purple
Green/Blue/Black   Green/Brown/Purple
Green/Blue/Purple

Green/Orange/Black   Green/Black/Purple
Green/Orange/Purple

Blue/Brown/Yellow   Blue/Yellow/Orange   Blue/Orange/Black
Blue/Brown/Orange   Blue/Yellow/Black   Blue/Orange/Purple
Blue/Brown/Black   Blue/Yellow/Purple
Blue/Brown/Purple

Blue/Black/Purple

Brown/Yellow/Orange   Brown/Orange/Black   Brown/Black/Purple
Brown/Yellow/Black   Brown/Orange/Purple
Brown/Yellow/Purple

Yellow/Orange/Black   Yellow/Black/Purple
Yellow/Orange/Purple

Orange/Black/Purple

Page 93
(Line totals: 1, 2, 4, 8, 16, 32, 64, 128, 256, 512, 1024)

Next five lines:

1, 11, 55, 165, 330, 462, 462, 330, 165, 55, 11, 1

1, 12, 66, 220, 495, 792, 924, 792, 495, 220, 66, 12, 1

1, 13, 78, 286, 715, 1287, 1716, 1716, 1287, 715, 286, 78, 13, 1

1, 14, 91, 364, 1001, 2002, 3003, 3432, 3003, 2002, 1001, 364, 91, 14, 1

1, 15, 105, 455, 1365, 3003, 5005, 6435, 6435, 5005, 3003, 1365, 455, 105, 15, 1